Historic Coker Hills

A Botanists' Neighborhood in Chapel Hill

Jill Ridky-Blackburn

Second Printing, 2019

Copyright © 2016 by Jill Ridky-Blackburn

All rights reserved.

Design and production by Rachel Loftis and Kiss Kreativ Design.
Cover art by Judith Smith.
Cover design by Shelly Hehenberger.
Published by the Chapel Hill Historical Society

COKER HILLS BOOK DONORS

The Chapel Hill Historical Society is grateful to the following donors whose generous support made this publication possible.

SPONSORS

Thomas S. Kenan
Joe W. Grisham in Memory of Evelyn M. Grisham

BENEFACTOR

Eugene McDonald

PATRONS

Joel Fleishman
Rudy and Eve Juliano
Brian and Moyra Kileff

Bruce Maggs
Chas and Judith Smith
Clay and Neva Whybark

DONORS

Elizabeth Cogswell Baskin
Sylvia Clements in Memory of John Belton Clements, Coker Hills Resident 1962-2014
Coker Hills Neighborhood Association
Thomas and Shauna Farmer
Chloe Seymore and Harrison Haynes

Mary Coker Joslin
Paul and Ave Lachiewicz
Bill and Erin Langston
Leon Edward Meyers
Oxide Architecture & Oxide Structure
Billy and Nancy Royal
Mary Avery Whittier

FRIENDS

Tina and Jerry Bell
Alan and Carolyn Brookhart
Mike and Julie Byerley
Fitch Lumber Company
Rob and Karen Futch
The Gastineaus
Jill Goldman
Rebecca Ho
Genevieve Jansen
Janet Kagan

Fred Lampe
Donna Lloyd
Gail Gillespie and Dwight Rogers
James and Joan Rose
David and Carol Rugen
Carlos and Kristina Sandi
The Sears
Harvey Wagner

CONTENTS

Acknowledgements   vii

Foreword   xi

1: Before Coker Hills   1
2: The Coker of Coker Hills   23
3: The Beginning of Coker Hills   41
4: Coker Hills Architects, Builders and Homes   89
5: The Coker Hills Legacy   181
6: Growing Up in Coker Hills   199
7: Neighborhood Advocacy   211

Afterword   227

About the Chapel Hill Historical Society   231

Appendices   233

Acknowledgements

I am of the opinion that my life belongs to the whole community, and as long as I live, it is my privilege to do for it whatever I can. I want to be thoroughly used up when I die, for the harder I work, the more I live.
— George Bernard Shaw

Many people contributed their time, effort, memories, recollections, anecdotes and personal knowledge of Coker Hills' history. Their contributions brought to light the historical significance of this neighborhood. While working on this project, I was fortunate to meet and work with many wonderful people, who gladly gave of their time and knowledge. I hesitate to list names for fear of unintentionally omitting someone. Those of you who helped know who you are. Your interests and efforts are greatly appreciated. However, at the risk of leaving out a very important name (the reader's perhaps), I do feel obligated to thank the following individuals:

First, the late William and Mary Coker Joslin, for invitations to their home and their willingness to share memories about Uncle Will (Dr. Coker) and to read drafts of several chapters. A thank you also to their daughter, Nell Joslin, who was encouraging and supportive. I will be forever appreciative of George Smart, Chair and Executive Director of North Carolina Modernist Houses, who provided affirmation and enthusiasm for the project, as well as a grant, just when it was most needed.

Special appreciation to: Tom Alexander- Holy Trinity Lutheran Church, Phil Bradley- NC Geologic Survey, Michael Burton- Orange County Land Records, Mark Chilton and staff- Register of Deeds Orange County, Mary Ann Coons- Earlham College, Ernest Dollar- City of Raleigh Museum and Pope

House Museum, Tom Driscoll- Naturalist, Richard Ellington- Chapel Hill Historical Society, Virginia Faust, Christian Hirni- Orange County Ranger, Myrick Howard- Preservation North Carolina, Joseph J. Kalo, IV, Tiletha Lane and Norah Wofford- Coker College, Donna Lloyd, Tom Magnuson- Founder of Trading Path Association, Joseph Marcus- Lady Bird Johnson Wildflower Center, Carol Ann McCormick- University of North Carolina Chapel Hill Herbarium, Roger Nelsen- UNC General Alumni Association, Robert (Bob)Page, Lisa Pearson- Arnold Arboretum of Harvard University, Mary Sonis- Naturalist, Ken Stewart- University of North Carolina Department of Geology, Angela Todd- Hunt Institute for Botanical Documentation, Pittsburgh, Pennsylvania, Meredith Tozzer- UNC General Alumni Association, Peter White- North Carolina Botanical Garden, Justin Williams- Hunt Institute for Botanical Documentation, Carnegie Mellon University, Susan Worley- Chapel Hill Historical Society and the wonderful staff at the University of North Carolina Wilson Library Southern Collection.

This book would not have been possible without information from original, former, and current neighbors and friends: The Bells, Sylvia Clements, Joel Fleishman, Gail Gillespie, The Glenns, Sylvia Hubbard, Genie Jansen, Nell Laton, The Prazmas, Dr. Billy Royal, The Sears, Betsy Summer, Susan Strobel, Rollie Tillman, the late Chris Waddell Nutter, Caroline and Bob Ward, The Warrens, Louanne Breslin Warren, Mary Whittier, Johnsie Wilkins, Susan Worley and Ida Wysor.

Great appreciation to the writers, editors, designers, and photographers including: Laura Cotterman, Dick Blackburn, Chase Hanes, Shelly Hehenberger, Edward Donald Kennedy, Patty Krebs, Rachel Loftis, Maximillian Longley, and Toby and Katherine Savage.

Special recognition to talented artist, neighbor and friend, Judith Smith, who designed and painted the beautiful cover for the book, capturing the blend of our modernist and traditional homes nestled within our natural world.

And finally, love to my family for being patient and understanding as I worked on this project. The dining room table will soon be available for meals. Deo gratias.

Foreword

Lying at the eastern edge of Chapel Hill, North Carolina, the Coker Hills neighborhood holds wonderful secrets. In this quiet and spacious landscape lies the story of Chapel Hill's rich cultural and natural history. To get a complete sense of the neighborhood and its landscape, one must strip away the roads and houses to look at the very earth beneath.

When University of North Carolina at Chapel Hill botany professor William C. Coker purchased the hilly area now known as Coker Hills, he bought it with a keen eye for the flora and the dramatic rises. Coker had transformed the land around his North Street home into a veritable Garden of Eden by planting a vast array of native and exotic plants. He may have had the same idea in mind for this tract overlooking the waters of Booker Creek.

Professor Coker shared his deep interest in plants of the area with another scientist and professor who had preceded him at the University by a century. Professor Elisha Mitchell, whose name later was given to the highest mountain in North Carolina (indeed, the highest point east of the Mississippi), often packed up his notebook and specimen bag and took off to tromp the fields and creek corridors surrounding Chapel Hill, recording the plants he found. On one trip in 1828, Mitchell wrote in his diary about finding *Carex acuta*, commonly called slim sedge, in the damp areas along Booker Creek. As the curious professor explored this stretch of creek, he may have known that he was following in the footsteps of the area's earliest settlers.

Along the edge of the Coker Hills neighborhood ran what

was simply known as "the Great Road." It stretched to Petersburg, Virginia and was one of several original roads that intersected at a small hilltop Episcopal church known as New Hope Chapel, from which the name Chapel Hill was derived. Today, Old Oxford Road is a shadow of this old trail that brought European settlers into the backcountry of Carolina in the eighteenth century. Before that, roads were simply footpaths made centuries earlier by nomadic Native Americans as they developed trade networks across North Carolina. One of the first settlers to arrive on the Great Road was Mark Morgan, whose family made the trek from Virginia in the early 1740s. And one of the earliest people to own the future site of Coker Hills was a Morgan son, John, who sold the land to John Craig in November 1811.

We can imagine turning back the pages of the past even further. Visualize standing on the highest point of Coker Hills, the end of a long east-west ridge, from which there is a view of the sun rising over a massive lake stretching from present-day Chapel Hill to Cary, North Carolina. Two hundred million years ago, Coker Hills was beachfront property overlooking a giant Triassic lake-a result of great upheaval in the earth's changing crust. From the rocks that remain, we can read at least some of the geological history of the dramatic landscape that William Coker acquired in the twentieth century. Soon nature would not be the only force altering the scene.

Upon Coker's death in 1953, ownership of the land transferred, according to his will, to Coker College, a South Carolina school started by his Civil War veteran father. The college hired a former student and then fellow botany professor of Coker's, Dr. Roland Totten, to develop the tract. The earliest houses began to spring up in the early 1960s; they would be as unique as the land upon which they sat.

The great social changes that America was experiencing

in the 1960s and 70s found their way into architecture. Young architects, like many who trained at the School of Design at North Carolina State University, embraced Modernism, a more organic style that broke from the aesthetic strictures of the past. In Chapel Hill, these architects found a blank canvas for their art. One, Arthur Cogswell, began working in the new Coker Hills development in the early 1960s, and his designs helped reshape the university town's vision of what homes could look like. Many of these homes forged a harmonious link between architecture and nature. Demand for Modernist houses grew until North Carolina had the third largest concentration of Modernist houses in the United States.

Today, those who live in Coker Hills are proud of their neighborhood and are eager to see it preserved. In 2007, residents petitioned the town for a Neighborhood Conservation District Plan to help keep the land and the character of their community safe. This book takes another step to ensure that the story of this land and its homes lives on. Recounting the facts, telling the stories, and retracing the steps of those who came before-all serve to educate the present and preserve it for the future.

Ernest Dollar
Executive Director, City of Raleigh Museum and Pope House Museum
Former Executive Director, Preservation Chapel Hill

1//Before Coker Hills

A nation that destroys its soils destroys itself. Forests are the lungs of our land, purifying the air and giving fresh strength to our people.
— Franklin D. Roosevelt

I think having land and not ruining it is the most beautiful art that anybody could ever want to own. — Andy Warhol

Before there were homes and streets, what would we have experienced and seen? What would the earliest inhabitants of the area have found? What would their natural habitat have been like: the geology, geography, flora, fauna, and wildlife? While we can never know exactly, with the help of some wonderful historians, scientists, naturalists, books, records and folk memories, we can paint a picture of what they may have seen or experienced, and identify what remains in Coker Hills to this day.

Geography and Geology
We cannot take one step in geology without drawing upon the fathomless stores of by-gone time. — Adam Sedgwick

Chapel Hill and the Coker Hills neighborhood are both located in the southeastern part of Orange County, North Carolina, near the eastern edge of the Piedmont physiographic province. No large streams originating in other counties cross through Orange County; rather the county serves as the upper watershed for three of North Carolina's major river systems (the Roanoke, the Neuse, and the Cape Fear). The landscape of Coker Hills and much of Orange County consists of broad upland ridges, gently rolling hills, and streams that cut relatively narrow valleys. Coker Hills drains generally to the southeast and ultimately into the Jordan Lake impoundment and the Cape Fear River. There are no natural lakes in Coker Hills or in the county. The neighborhood and most of Chapel Hill sit on what geologists call the Piedmont Upland, as opposed to the nearby Triassic Lowland. Soils of the Piedmont Upland are generally acidic and derive from metamorphosed volcanic and igneous rocks (collectively these rocks comprise the Carolina Terrane, formerly referred to as the Carolina Slate Belt). The humid climate of the Piedmont, which receives approximately 45 inches of rain a year, speeds the chemical breakdown and erosion of rock. Rocks in this area are typically quite weathered.[1]

To the west and north of Chapel Hill, a monadnock (an isolated hill) known as Bald Mountain (elevation: 762 feet) is at the headwaters of Bolin Creek. This stream eventually drains the Coker Hills neighborhood as it flows east along the neighborhood's southern edge. A second stream, Booker Creek, also drains the area as it flows east and south to join with Bolin Creek just east of US 501 North (Fordham Blvd.). While flowing on the Piedmont Upland and through the Coker Hills area, Bolin Creek has a downward gradient of about 40 feet per mile. This creates a faster water velocity and more erosive flow, but when the stream reaches the University Place area, the gradient drops to 5 feet per mile. This change reflects the fact that in the vicinity of East Franklin Street, the stream enters the Triassic Lowland (geologically, the Durham Triassic Basin), where softer sedimentary rocks allow for more stream meandering and the development of a broader floodplain. This drastic change in

---

[1] Philip J. Bradley, "A Geologic Adventure along the Eno River," *Information Circular 35* (Raleigh: NC Department of Environment and Natural Resources), 2007, 3.

gradient and consequent slowing of the water is the major reason there is the potential for flooding in the Eastgate/Fordham Boulevard area during periods of heavy rain. As Booker Creek joins Bolin, it becomes Little Creek, which continues flowing south to Jordan Lake.

The illustration shows the change in topography from Coker Hills, on the Piedmont Upland, to the Triassic Lowland in the University Place area.

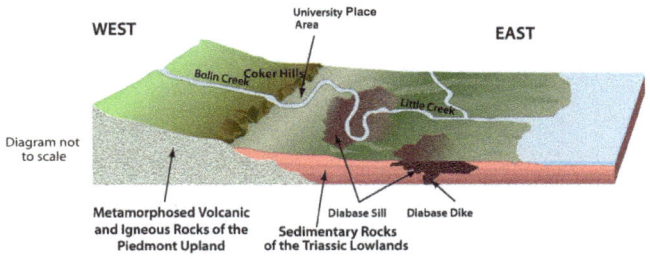

Piedmont Upland and Triassic Lowlands
Source: Phil Bradley, North Carolina

Although it is difficult to imagine, more than 630 million years ago the land that eventually became North Carolina consisted of a chain of volcanic islands off the coast of ancient Africa. The islands eventually collided and became part of the ancient North American continent. North Carolina geologist Phil Bradley observes that modern volcanoes and their deposits provide guidance to understanding the geologic history of North Carolina. He notes that metamorphosed volcanic and plutonic igneous rocks underlie the Coker Hills area. Volcanic rock is formed when hot lava erupts out of a volcanic vent or when lava explodes from volcanoes; plutonic rock forms when magma cools and solidifies underground without ever erupting. Common rock types formed by solidified magma are called granodiorite or granite.

Today, granodiorite can be observed on walks through Coker Hills, for example, on the left along the school path from Curtis Road toward Estes Hills Elementary School.

Granodiorite
Photo by Jill Blackburn

Rock fragments composed of quartz are also common in Coker Hills. This white quartz formed when boiling water, containing dissolved silicon and oxygen, forced its way into cracks in the igneous rock and then precipitated out to become quartz as it cooled. These quartz veins are abundant in the Carolina Terrane, and because quartz is resistant to weathering, the surrounding volcanic rock often erodes more quickly leaving a string of quartz pebbles and boulders. Quartz fragments in Coker Hills range from small, gravel-sized pieces to much larger boulder-sized blocks.

White Opaque Quartz
Photo by Jill Blackburn

Trading Paths and Early Settlement
Being aware of history makes you a part of the place you live in; history provides a sense of continuity. — Tom Magnuson

Orange County, North Carolina, was founded in 1752 and named for William V of Orange, the grandson of King George II of England. Orange County was an ideal environment for early settlers. Valleys provided fertile soil, and water was in abundant supply with New Hope Creek, the Haw, Eno, Little, and Flat Rivers and all of their tributaries. "Throughout all of this territory except on the poorer ridges, the forest growth was magnificent, with the oaks predominating. The soil was ideal for the flourishing growth of hardwoods and deciduous trees. Oaks four feet in diameter at their base were not uncommon, and occasional specimens six feet in diameter were found. Along the streams, these oaks and hickories, birches, beeches, poplars and sycamores towered high, and the elm and the maple attained unusual size and magnificence of foliage. . . All this territory was a paradise for the hunter and trapper, abounding in bear, deer, beaver, wild turkey, and all the smaller varieties of game. It was the habitat and hunting grounds for the Haw, the Eno, and the Occoneechee Indians."[2] In 2004, when the Love House at 410 East Franklin Street was renovated, Native American artifacts dating from 800 BC to 800 CE were discovered. In the early 1960's, an artifact was found in Coker Hills by the Masson daughters, (Michelle Masson and Karen Masson Kendig) when excavation for the in-ground pool at the Cogswell House at 308 North Elliott Road was completed. The young sisters wandered over to the excavation site and found an item believed to be an "arrowhead".

State Archaeologist, Stephen R. Claggett, classified the "arrowhead" as a Guilford Point, which was probably used as a spear point and/or knife but not as an arrowhead. Such items were made and used by Indians before they started to use bows and arrows. Claggett estimates the Guilford point to be about 6,000 years old, based on the excavation and dating of similar points from several sites across the Piedmont. The point is made from a type of volcanic rock, generally called rhyolite. The name of the native "tribe" that made such items is not known due to its great age, but they were definitely ancestors of the Eno, Occoneechee, Saxapahaw and related to groups who were here when the first Europeans entered their territory in the 17th and early 18th centuries. The Guilford Point found in Coker Hills shows signs of having been re-sharpened (by chipping/flaking) along most of its edges. This was quite common for Guilford points and was likely done several times before the piece was discarded and replaced by a newer implement.

---

[2] *Francis Nash, "The History of Orange County" (Raleigh, NC: The North Carolina Society, Daughters of the American Revolution), NC Booklet Vol. X, No.2, October 1910, 58–59.*

Guilford Point
Photo by Karen Masson Kendig

Before the founding of the University of North Carolina at Chapel Hill in 1789, the area which was to become Chapel Hill was simply referred to as "the crossroads," identifying a series of paths that crossed near a chapel. Tom Magnuson, founder of the Trading Path Association, whose mission is to preserve, promote and study the historic Trading Path of the Southeastern Piedmont, has identified old trading paths that probably existed prior to the 1700s, stretching from Virginia to Georgia. The oldest ones are hard-packed footpaths, located below the ridgeline. The footpaths were likely created by Native Americans who knew that walking below a ridgeline screened their movements from potential enemies.

In the vicinity of Coker Hills, there was an old pathway known as the Old Oxford Highway or University Road. The original path was laid down on high ground and used as a wagon road. Later, apparently to make travel more convenient for Duncan Cameron, one of the University of North Carolina's first trustees, who lived at Farintosh in Durham County, an improved roadway was built. In the 1790s, "the University Road," from Durham to Chapel Hill was probably a combination of dirt and cobble with a wet ford across New Hope Creek. Today, Old Oxford Road and Erwin Road are in line with the original wagon road. In fact, part of the old roadbed is visible in the area around the Chapel Hill Public Library. Tom Magnuson believes that part of the old University Road and Trading Path would have crossed through Coker Hills. These old paths become unidentifiable as new roads and homes are built, but during a visit to the neighborhood, Magnuson observed areas off North Elliott Road and Old Oxford Road that showed signs of being part of this trading path.

Flora, Fauna, and Wildlife
Nature did all things well. — Michelangelo

The woods to be found in and around Coker Hills today include remnants of the two most common natural types in Orange County: Mesic Mixed Hardwood forest and Dry-Mesic Oak–Hickory forest. The nearby Battle Park, a preserved natural area, consists primarily of these two natural types.

However, over the centuries, extensive land clearing took place in the Piedmont for farming and timber. Even before European settlements, Native Americans in the area may have used controlled burning to maintain optimal conditions for game and agriculture. By the time the Europeans arrived in the 1700s, there was a mosaic of forests and open savanna-like areas. From the middle 1700s into the twentieth century, North Carolina supplied timber for the shipbuilding, construction, railroad, and furniture industries.

Carrboro played a significant role in the early timber industry. The town, first known as West End, provided a railroad depot for the University. The population increased in West End in 1878 when Thomas Lloyd built a steam-powered grist mill near the train depot. This would become the Alberta Cotton Mill (today Carr Mill Mall), and in 1900 the town was briefly called

Lloydville in his honor. In 1911, the town was renamed Venable in honor of chemistry professor and University of North Carolina President Francis Preston Venable. In that same year, Julius Shakespeare Carr, a tobacco industrialist, bought the mill and other nearby buildings from Lloyd. In 1914, the town was renamed Carrboro, after Carr, who had expanded the mill and also provided electrical power to the citizens. In addition to the textile mills and the railroad depot, Carrboro served the timber industry. By the 1920's and 1930's, Carrboro was the largest producer of railroad crossties on the East Coast.

Orange County Ranger, Christian Hirni, of the North Carolina Forest Service, visited Coker Hills and shared some interesting insights regarding the trees found in the neighborhood. Today, ninety percent of the trees in Coker Hills are less than 100 years old, suggesting that this land was cleared for agriculture, timber production and the neighborhood development. Most of the pines in Coker Hills are loblolly, a species with a typical life span of 80 years, though they can live up to 125 years. Additional neighborhood trees identified include sourwood, sweet gum, beech, elm, oak and tulip poplar. These species are usually found in secondary or successional forests, needing full sun to grow.

Ranger Hirni believes that trees logged in Carrboro, Hillsborough, and most likely Coker Hills supplied the crosstie mill in Carrboro. Wood used for crossties typically came from sweet gums and pines. In the late 1980s, an item resembling a horseshoe was found buried in the ground off Lyons Road. Naturalist Mary Sonis identified the item as a mule shoe, an opinion supported by farrier Chip Crumbly. Crumbly thought the shoe might be an old Phoenix Company mule shoe (made in Poughkeepsie, New York) from the 1930s or earlier. In the South, mules continued to be used as a form of farm power far longer than in other parts of the country, especially on smaller farms and for market gardens. The mule shoe suggests mules were used for farming and to haul timber. Mule shoes and horseshoes have also been found near homes on Audubon Road. In addition, Dr. Henry Totten (botanist and land agent of Coker Hills) noted in his correspondence that he had seen evidence of old logging trails on the Coker Hills property.

Mule Shoe
Photo by Jill Blackburn

The Bells, original Coker Hills owners, recalled that soon after their family moved into their new home on Michaux Road, the first snowfall revealed old plant furrows on their property. Caroline Ward, another original owner on Michaux, remembered scrub pine growth on some of the surrounding undeveloped lots and some areas with furrows from days when the land was farmed.

All of the plants on the land contributed to the health of the ecosystem. Native plants helped to sustain native butterflies, insects, birds, mammals, reptiles, and other native species. Trees like the beech, oak and hickory would have provided nesting habitats for birds as well as acorns and nuts for the wildlife. In the winter, native evergreens provided shelter and food. Migrating birds relied on insects in the woods to sustain them during their long-distance flights. They also counted on energy from the fruits of the flowering dogwoods and other trees and shrubs.

There are many wildflowers and plants that would have been seen on this land. Some of these native plants can still be found today in the neighborhood, including ferns, Little Brown Jug, and Jack in the Pulpit. Native plants like Black-eyed Susan, Phlox, and Aster all contributed to the sustainability and beauty of the natural environment.

If we had been here before the American Revolution, according to the late John Terres, a naturalist who spent the better part of the 1960s observing wildlife in and around Chapel Hill, we would have seen "flocks of wild turkeys. The turkeys would feed on acorns from the dominant oaks: the post oak, white oak and black oak, and the fruits of the flowering dogwoods and other plants of the oak-hickory forest."[3]

Wild Turkey
Photo by Mary Sonis

Mary Sonis notes that the land would have been home to many birds and continues to provide a habitat for many species of birds and other animals. She too believes that there once would

---

[3] *John Terres, From Laurel Hill to Siler's Bog (Chapel Hill: The University of North Carolina Press, 1993), 6.*

have been Wild Turkeys and perhaps Northern Bobwhites, a species in decline today, though efforts are being made to reintroduce it at the nearby Mason Farm Biological Reserve.

Red-tailed Hawk
Photo by Mary Sonis

Tom Driscoll, a local ornithologist and president of the New Hope Chapter of the National Audubon Society (representing Chatham, Durham, and Orange counties), recently commented on the variety of birds to be found in the neighborhood. He suggests that Coker Hills encompasses a typical "urban forest habitat" of the central North Carolina Piedmont. However, because there are still pockets of well-established forests with extensive, older deciduous trees and conifers, birds not commonly seen near houses, such as warblers, can be observed. Even larger birds of prey and scavenging birds make their way to Coker Hills. Turkey Vultures and Black Vultures can be seen flying over the area. Hawks to be found here include the Cooper's Hawk, Red-shouldered Hawk, and Red-tailed Hawk. In fact, the first two hawks in this list have actually nested in Coker Hills. Cooper's Hawks eat smaller birds, so they are sometimes seen hunting near bird feeders. The large, stocky, grey-brown Barred Owl can be seen and heard in the evening or early morning hours. Eastwood Lake and Bolin Creek provide a prime habitat for owls nesting in the thick groves of trees.

Barred Owl
Photo by Mary Sonis

Mourning Doves are commonly heard and sometimes seen on overhead wires as well as at bird feeders. Red-bellied and Downy Woodpeckers are common, and the Hairy Woodpecker and Northern Flicker can be seen on occasion. The large and splendid Pileated Woodpecker also resides in Coker Hills. All of these woodpeckers most likely nest here as well, and many come to bird feeders, especially when suet is offered. The Eastern Phoebe, a type of flycatcher, can often be seen swinging its tail and singing its name ("phoe-be; phoe-be").

Downy Woodpecker
Photo by Mary Sonis

Many birds that nest in Coker Hills can be seen and heard year-round and are frequent visitors to bird feeders. These include the Blue Jay, American Crow, Tufted Titmouse, Carolina Chickadee, and the White-breasted Nuthatch. The Brown-headed Nuthatch can be found in pine trees but is less common in the area.

Carolina Wrens are noisy, little brown birds that are commonly found around Coker Hills homes throughout the year. American Robins will be seen pulling up earthworms and Eastern Bluebirds will visit feeders, especially when suet and/or peanuts are available. Brown Thrashers and Pine Warblers will also visit more often when suet is offered. Pine Warblers can be seen all year in Coker Hills; they nest in the pine trees.

In Coker Hills, it is also common to see Northern Mockingbirds and Brown Thrashers. European Starlings, introduced from Europe, are sometimes seen in Coker Hills, especially near the Estes Hills Elementary School. They probably nest in the area and will also come to bird feeders.

Eastern Towhees nest in the area and will regularly visit bird feeders, as do Chipping and Song Sparrows. Northern

Cardinals, the state bird of North Carolina, are common at feeders, especially when sunflower seeds are available. House Finches commonly nest in Coker Hills, especially near Estes Hills Elementary and Phillips Middle Schools and will readily come to bird feeders. American Goldfinches, bright yellow birds common in Coker Hills, nest in this area and visit bird feeders, especially when nyjer seed is offered. Wood Ducks, Mallards, Canadian Geese, Great Blue Herons, and Ring-billed Gulls visit nearby Eastwood Lake and can be seen flying over Coker Hills; but they don't reside or nest in the neighborhood.

As with any region, there is seasonal variation in bird life. The North Carolina Piedmont is on the Atlantic Flyway, a north-south migratory path, so some birds who are not year-round residents can be seen in Coker Hills during spring and fall migrations. For example, Carolina Chickadees are year-round residents, whereas White-throated Sparrows are here only in winter. Other winter residents include the Yellow-bellied Sapsucker, Red-breasted Nuthatch, and the Hermit Thrush. Ruby-crowned and Golden-crowned Kinglets are tiny birds that spend the winter in this area, and Cedar Waxwings can be seen in large flocks of up to 100 birds eating berries from holly bushes or junipers.

Yellow-rumped Warblers are commonly seen in Coker Hills in the winter and will come to bird feeders where suet is offered. White-throated Sparrows, Dark-eyed Juncos, Purple Finches (similar to House Finches), Pine Siskins, and American Gold-finches will migrate to this area periodically and can also be seen in Coker Hills.

Birds seen only in the summer usually migrate here to nest and will return south after nesting. Chimney Swifts return in the spring and frequently can be seen flying over Coker Hills. They often nest in the Estes Hills Elementary School chimney, but typically leave the area in late October. Ruby-throated Hummingbirds return in the spring and can be seen through September in Coker Hills. They nest here and are attracted to red flowers and hummingbird feeders.

Great Crested Flycatchers also return in the spring and can be seen through September. They nest in Coker Hills as well. Acadian Flycatchers return each spring and nest along Booker and Bolin creeks. Their call, which sounds like "peet-sah," can often be heard, though they are rarely seen. Red-eyed Vireos return each spring and can be heard calling all day long. They nest in Coker Hills and usually leave in September. Other vireos, such as the Yellow-throated Vireo and Blue-headed Vireo, can be seen in Coker Hills during migration but are not common species here. Fish Crows return to the area in the spring and stay until late fall. They are very similar to the American Crow, although somewhat smaller. They have two calls, both distinct from the American Crow's familiar "caw." The Fish Crow has a nasal "kwok" and a two-noted "ah-ah." They visit bird feeders as well.

Nuthatch
Photo by Mary Sonis

Yellow-billed Cuckoos are often heard but rarely seen in the neighborhood, though some may nest in Coker Hills. House Wrens are commonly seen from spring through September. They are somewhat smaller and plainer than Carolina Wrens. Another tiny bird that migrates to Coker Hills is the Blue-Gray Gnatcatcher, arriving early in the spring and visible until September.

Yellow-billed Cuckoo
Photo by Mary Sonis

Wood Thrushes arrive in the spring and spend the summer nesting in this area. They prefer the thickly-wooded forest areas in Coker Hills. Other types of thrushes, such as Veeries, can sometimes be seen in Coker Hills, but only during spring or fall migration. Gray Catbirds migrate here in spring and stay until September.

Warblers, except for the Pine and Yellow-rumped Warbler, are rarely seen outside of migration times, when they are heading north or south. However, there are several species of wood warblers that may reside in Coker Hills during the summer and probably nest here, including the American Redstart, Ovenbird (a warbler that nests on the ground and builds a nest that looks like a Dutch oven), Hooded Warbler, Black-and-white Warbler, and the Northern Parula.

Summer and Scarlet Tanagers and the Common Grackle are seen in Coker Hills and probably nest in the area. Brown-headed Cowbirds are common during the spring/summer nesting season. Cowbirds, commonly seen at bird feeders, lay their eggs in other birds' nests, and the other birds raise the cowbirds' young.

Coker Hills is fortunate to have such a varied bird population, although only the more regularly observed birds have been noted here. Other birds may briefly appear during times of migration or unusual weather events (for instance, after a hurricane). The New Hope Audubon Society (www.newhopeaudubon.org) is a wonderful resource to learn more about birds in Coker Hills and the local area.

Eastern Box Turtle
Photo by Gail Gillespie

Reptiles and amphibians, in particular, salamanders, were probably plentiful in the area before the Coker Hills neighborhood was developed. Reptiles and amphibians that may be seen today include the Eastern Fence Lizard, Five-lined Skink,

Brown Snake, Worm Snake, Black Rat Snake, Copperhead, American Toad, Gray Tree Frog, and the Slimy Salamander.

The Eastern Box Turtle (*Terrapene carolina carolina*), photographed on Audubon Road in Coker Hills, is the state reptile and the only land turtle in North Carolina. This treasure of the southern woods can live in the wild for over 100 years but less than a few months in captivity. Like many creatures, they are vulnerable to anthropogenic or human-induced mortality (cars, equipment, etc.). They should never be relocated, since they will continue to try to wander back to find their home territory. They mature slowly and begin to breed at age seven. Males have red eyes and females brown. At one time they were plentiful across the entire east coast, but now they are a rare find in New England. Although still common in North Carolina, their population is in decline in many areas of the state, including Orange Country.

The native Gray Fox would have been present before houses were built and still is today, although in diminished numbers. The newest animal addition to this area is the Eastern Coyote. At one time, coyotes were only encountered in Canada and the American West. Now these carnivores can be found along the east coast and down to South Carolina.

Beavers were extirpated from North Carolina by the beginning of the twentieth century, but the species was reintroduced in the 1930s with beavers brought in from Pennsylvania. In fact, some years ago there was a beaver family living near Umstead Park, upstream on Bolin Creek. Beavers have also been sighted at Eastwood Lake, adjacent to the Coker Hills neighborhood. Beavers have created some problems in town when their dams block the streams and create local flooding.

Wolves, cougars, bobcats, and even bears likely lived in the forests of this part of the Piedmont in years past. These predators kept the White-tailed Deer population within the limits of the deer's forest food supply. When deer were scarce, predators most likely took raccoon, opossum, fox, squirrel, rabbit, shrew, and chipmunk. Today, these "prey" species continue to live on this land, particularly the ever-increasing deer population, while most of the predators have been forced to find other areas for hunting. Coker Hills has experienced an increased deer population and even has a "neighborhood" Albino Deer.

Coker Hills Albino Deer
Photo by Mary Sonis

A survey of natural and wildlife habitats for Orange County found that half of the fifty-three natural areas identified in Orange County are located in the southeastern quarter of the county (the Chapel Hill area). This is also the area that is "the most heavily populated and shows the most probability of further, accelerated suburban development. It is ironic that the most geologically and topographically diverse part of the county is also the one in which the pressure of habitat modification is the greatest."[4]

In Coker Hills and Chapel Hill, the pressure for development and re-development brings with it the potential to change the quality of life for humans and wildlife alike. "Clearing land, cutting trees, and draining wetlands put plants and animals at risk. It is important to remember that the effects of these activities on nature extend beyond the boundary of the clearing or disturbance. At the very least, clearing introduces light to areas that were once shaded, drastically altering microclimates. Predation by the introduction of larger numbers of domestic animals, i.e. cats and dogs, increases pressure on native animal populations."[5] Expanded road networks result in higher mortality for native animals and greater fragmentation of their natural habitats.

The need to balance pressures for further development against the desire to preserve natural resources and quality of all life remains an important issue for Coker Hills and the Chapel Hill area. Donald C. Peattie, American botanist, naturalist, and author, may have said it best: "Once they are gone, the trees and the grasslands, the screaming waterfowl, the beavers and the antelope, we can only remember them with longing. We are not God. We cannot make America over again as it was in the beginning, but we can come to what is left of our heritage with a patriot's reverence."[6]

---

[4] *Bruce Sorrie and Rich Shaw, "Inventory of Natural Areas and Wildlife Habitats for Orange County, North Carolina," (Orange County Environment & Resource Conservation Department, December 2004, Update of 1988 report by Dawson Sather and Stephen Hall).*
[5] *Ibid.*
[6] *Donald C. Peattie, The Road of a Naturalist, Trinity University Press, 2013, Chapter 9.*

2//The Coker of Coker Hills

His work stands as a living breathing monument to a man who is rich in ideas, brave, daring, venturing, quiet and unassuming in achieving.
— Lucy Lay, Alumni Review, 1926

William Chambers Coker*
1872-1953

The Coker Hills neighborhood is named for William Chambers Coker, born in Hartsville, South Carolina in 1872 to James Lide Coker and Susan Stout. The fourth of seven children, he was named after his mother's Uncle William and referred to as Will by the family. The Coker lineage began in South Carolina and can be traced back to the marriage of Caleb Coker (28 years old) and Hannah Lide (18 years old) in 1830. When they were married, Caleb and Hannah resided in Caleb's small three-room cottage in Society Hill, South Carolina. Caleb was a successful planter and merchant. Hannah and Caleb had ten children and their children were the sum and substance of their lives. Their

---

*Photo courtesy of the University of North Carolina Chapel Hill Herbarium

son, James, became the father of William Chambers Coker. James went to the South Carolina Military Academy, which later became known as the Citadel, in Charleston. James did not find life at the Academy congenial, and he wrote home saying it was as dull as ever and overladen with studies. In 1857, without a degree from the Academy, he spent an academic year at Harvard to study science and work in the chemistry laboratory. He studied under two highly-respected scientists of the day, botanist Asa Gray and Swiss-born naturalist Louis Agassiz. In 1858, James returned home with a box of scientific equipment and a plan to conduct further experiments in field and planting methods. James was successful with his agricultural work, but life changed during the Civil War. The Coker family suffered hardships and grieved for James' brother, who died during the war.[1]

As James worked to recover from the Civil War, he became convinced the South would have to develop a supplement to agriculture as a source of economic growth. In 1883, James took the lead in establishing the Darlington Manufacturing Company, and the company evolved into one of the largest employers in Hartsville.

James taught the family self-discipline, and this had a powerful impact on the development of his children. His oldest son, James Jr., and his youngest son, Charles, were both interested in inventions, engineering, manufacturing, and corporate management. Another son, David, was interested in agriculture as well as plant breeding and propagation. David worked toward developing more productive and disease-resistant seeds for cotton and other crops. His efforts led to the establishment of the

---

[1] *Much of the information for this chapter was derived from the following reference: Mary Coker Joslin, Essays on William Chambers Coker, Passionate Botanist (Chapel Hill: University of North Carolina at Chapel Hill Library, 2003).*

Coker Pedigreed Seed Company.

James was eager to share his enthusiasm for nature with his children and friends. During walks through the woods and fields near their home, he would call his children's attention to interesting natural phenomena. Son William Chambers Coker began to share his father's enthusiasm for nature at a young age. One of his earliest childhood memories was reading Darwin's *On the Origin of Species* that he found in his father's library. Later in life, he often spoke about the influence of his father's library and Darwin's writings on his ultimate career choice.

William Chambers Coker attended South Carolina College, later known as the University of South Carolina, and became a distinguished graduate, receiving his Bachelor of Science degree in 1894. The president of the college stated that Coker was "one of the ablest men we ever graduated," and according to his history professor, he was "a perfect gentleman . . . an earnest student . . . with a . . . bent for original investigation."[2] While at college, Coker tried to read excerpts from classic literature every day in addition to his regular assignments. This interest in the classics remained with him throughout his life.

After graduation, he joined the Atlantic National Bank in Wilmington, North Carolina. At that time the bank was one of the largest in the South. Although the bank president, J. Wilkins Norwood, was a friend of Coker's father, Coker's promotion to second vice president within his first two years at the bank was a function of his capability and hard work, not family friendship. Although he was a very successful banker, his passion was to study plants.

In 1898, at the age of 26, Coker was accepted into the botany graduate program at Johns Hopkins University. He was the first graduate student of Duncan Starr Johnson, the only professor of botany at Hopkins and just five years Coker's senior.

---

[2] *Ibid., pages 23 – 24.*

Coker's dissertation, concerning the seeds of the Bald Cypress, was completed in 1901 and became the first paper to be published by the Johns Hopkins Botanical Laboratories.

The Coker family and the Hartsville community were quite proud of his educational accomplishments. According to family legend, when he returned to Hartsville with his doctoral degree, he was greeted at the train station by the town band and a chorus singing, "Hail the Conquering Hero Comes." As the train pulled into the station, he realized he was about to be treated "like royalty," so he quickly made his way to the other side of the train to escape the fanfare.

Still eager to continue his research and interest in conifer seeds, Coker applied for and was awarded a postdoctoral position at Bonn University in Germany, working in the botanical laboratory of Professor Eduard Strasburger. On September 4, 1901, he sailed to Germany. While at Bonn, Coker's postdoctoral work attracted the attention of Dr. Francis Preston Venable, President of the University of North Carolina. President Venable had also studied at Bonn and had great respect for German-trained scholars. Henry V. P. Wilson, a biology professor at the University of North Carolina at Chapel Hill, also thought highly of Coker and his work. They had met earlier, when, during Coker's studies at Hopkins, he took a summer research position at a marine laboratory in Beaufort, North Carolina. During that summer, Coker enjoyed being back in the South and was excited to be working in Wilson's lab studying algae. Wilson appreciated Coker's good work while in Beaufort and hoped that Coker would one day come to Chapel Hill. In 1902, Professor Wilson wrote Coker in Bonn and offered him a position as an associate professor in the Biology Department with an annual salary of $1,000 but with no promise of a salary increase or promotion. Thus, at the relatively young age of 29,

Coker became the first botany professor in the University of North Carolina's Department of Biology. Over the next forty years, he would become internationally known for his studies of fungi and water molds (mycology). He also continued to publish research on seed development in conifers and studies of native trees, shrubs, vines, and herbaceous flora, and on practical landscaping. His published books include *The Plant Life of Hartsville* and *The Trees of North Carolina*, the latter co-authored with his former student, colleague, and friend H. R. Totten. Covering 51 years of research, Coker's writings include 137 publications.

In addition to being an avid writer, Coker also served as an editor and publisher. In 1904, he became the editor of the *Journal of the Elisha Mitchell Scientific Society*, a periodical first published in 1884 and renamed the *Journal of the North Carolina Academy of Science* in 2002. Coker wrote articles for the journal and served as its editor until 1945. He also solicited articles, supervised the printing and distribution to subscribers, and eventually assumed full editorial and production responsibilities.

In 1903, one year into Coker's faculty appointment, President Venable asked Coker to chair the University Buildings and Grounds Committee. In particular, he sought Coker's help to improve an area of campus commonly referred to as "a boggy pasture," an area which was known for being too wet and murky to be suitable for a university building. "The land was considered most unsightly and a useless bit of ground connected with the university."[3] But Coker saw the potential for something wonderful and spent several years designing, preparing, and then planting the area. Coker turned the "boggy pasture" into what is today the Coker Arboretum. With Coker's good work, the arboretum began with more than 400 species of plants. His favorite

---

[3] *Chapel Hill News*, "Out Town," Sunday, February 23, 2003, Section C.

tree in the arboretum was the Marshall's thorn (*Crataegus marshallii*) that bears white flowers in the spring and red fruit in the fall. The efforts of Coker and the Buildings and Grounds Committee were celebrated in the book *Look Homeward Angel,* in which author Thomas Wolfe described the charm of the University of North Carolina at Chapel Hill in springtime. The arboretum received attention outside of the state as well. A botany professor from the University of Illinois wrote to Coker and asked for more information about the arboretum. On July 28, 1917, Coker replied: "I may say that the main arboretum includes about five acres of ground, a part which is included by hedges and a medicinal garden. We also have a special garden for the shrubs of North Carolina, including about two acres. My principal object so far has been to get together the woody plants of North Carolina and to make the place of pleasing appearance as an object lesson for parks and home grounds."[4] In this letter he implies the arboretum is part of the university's effort to give helpful examples for the beautification of homes and communities. Later, Coker and others introduced exotic shrubs and trees to supplement his collection of native plants grown in the arboretum. As director of the arboretum, Coker shared plants he propagated with members of the local community. The following notice appeared in the *Chapel Hill News,* on November 18, 1918:

"Ornamental shrubs free of charge to persons in Chapel Hill interested in improving their yards by planting of shrubs. The University Arboretum will give free of charge a considerable collection of desirable plants. The plants will be for distribution to first comers-to those who apply at the Arboretum Saturday morning of this week. W.C. Coker, Director."[5]

---

[4] *Joslin, Essays on William Chambers Coker, 94.*
[5] *Ibid., 108.*

Regarding the arboretum, University of North Carolina Professor Archibald Henderson, in his history of the campus, wrote, "With hundreds of species of plants and trees artistically arranged for beauty and display, this is one of the most exquisite and harmonious naturalistic gardens in the United States. . . . With an abiding sense of beauty and a disciplined passion for adornment, Dr. Coker has taken the Campus and indeed the entire Chapel Hill area for his province."[6]

Marshall's thorn*

Coker was always eager to enhance the appearance of his home, neighborhood, and community. He believed attention to one's surroundings elevated the quality of life and had the power to improve the community, environment, and even one's personal outlook:

"When you see this great improvement already made, you will not be quite satisfied until you take down that old sagging fence and plant a hedge in its place. Then, as you grow in grace and in love of beauty, you will add shrubs to the corners and about the house, shape up the walks and keep them hoed, and screen the unsightly places with evergreen privets or mock oranges. . . . There will be joy in your heart at these transformations, and when, some day, you realize that the neighbors are trying to follow your example, your full reward will appear."[7]

---

[6] *Ibid., 100.*
[7] *Ibid., 110-11.*
**Courtesy Andy and Sally Wasowski, Lady Bird Johnson Wildflower Center*

In 1908, Coker was promoted to professor and chair of the newly-established Department of Botany. In that same year, he established the University of North Carolina Herbarium with an impressive collection of pressed, dried plant specimens. Coker spent a great deal of time collecting plant specimens in Chapel Hill, on his travels back home to Hartsville and throughout the country. On one occasion, while traveling with family members, he stopped the car, got out, and climbed down from a highway bridge into a bog to retrieve a prize specimen. His letters to friends, colleagues, and students included many inquiries trying to locate specimens for his collection. William R. Burk, retired University of North Carolina at Chapel Hill biology librarian, listed a total of twenty-nine plants named after Dr. Coker. Two examples, *Liatris cokeri* and *Lycopus cokeri*, are found only in North and South Carolina.

Liatris cokeri
Photo by Will Stuart

In 1920, Coker was awarded a Kenan Research Professorship for his many efforts and accomplishments, especially establishing the arboretum and herbarium. Today, the University of North Carolina Chapel Hill Herbarium is a part of the North

Carolina Botanical Garden and is considered the premier herbarium in the Southeast, used by students, botanists, taxonomists, and other professionals and contains more than 800,000 specimens of plants, fungi, and algae.

Coker continued his work with the University Buildings and Grounds Committee and developed the university's master building and landscape plan. He devoted countless hours to this effort, driven by the desire for the university to be viewed as one of the most notable institutions of education in the South. As a result, Coker befriended John Nolen, the city planner of Cambridge, Massachusetts. Nolen was a former student of Frederick Law Olmsted, who is considered the father of American landscape architecture, gaining notoriety for co-designing many urban parks, including Central Park in New York City. Coker and Nolen corresponded for almost three years discussing the university plan and implementation. On March 14, 1917, Coker wrote to Nolen asking for a definite plan for the grounds of the university in which he would locate all buildings, roads, and paths and requested a date for Nolen to visit the campus. In a letter dated May 14, 1918, from Coker to H.R. Totten (Totten was then serving in the Army), Coker mentions the completion of the plan and the prospect of a new quadrangle extending southward from South Building, with a gymnasium at the end and dormitories on the sides. Coker worked closely on the plans with University President Edward Kidder Graham and Dean of the College of Liberal Arts Marvin H. Stacy. When Graham and Stacy died suddenly in late 1918 and early 1919, respectively, Coker inherited the entire responsibility for the university's evolving campus plan.

The Nolen plan, dated February 26, 1919, showed all of the existing buildings with fourteen new ones proposed. The plan retained the proposal for a great rectangular area south of South

Building, which would eventually be enclosed at the southern end by the Louis Round Wilson Library. Today, Polk Place, with its spacious lawns and double rows of oaks extending between the two distinguished buildings, is much appreciated by both the campus community and visitors.

Coker continued to be concerned with campus improvement and wrote to the new university president, H. W. Chase, on April 30, 1920, asking to be given authority to act in the interest of campus improvement. Again on June 9, he wrote to President Chase, saying, "At present the University forests, including Battle Park, are being badly neglected with the result there is much ill treatment and abuse. I suggest the care of these adjacent woods be placed in the hands of one you think fit, with the power to keep them in reasonable order and to enforce certain regulations as to their use."[8]

Coker maintained an ongoing concern for the proper maintenance and protection of the campus and especially the arboretum. In a letter he sent to the director of the university's summer school on June 28, 1920, he complained that summer school students were injuring the arboretum's plants for the sake of romance: "The regular term students, who have learned something of University ways, very rarely cause any trouble in the Arboretum, but . . . the temporary students cause considerable damage by picking almost any flowers, apparently, that they want."[9]

Coker's countless hours consulting with well-known architects and developing landscape proposals resulted in the flourishing of one of the most beautiful university campuses in the country. Coker provided the university, town, and state with half a century of attention and care for natural beauty, and, in fact, he considered himself a public servant to the state. He described the physical environment of Chapel Hill this way:

---

[8] Ibid., 99.
[9] Ibid., 94.

"Nothing could so distinguish us as the presence of these trees . . . in their possession we stand without rival among the colleges of the country."[10] R.W. Madry, in a newspaper article dated August 26, 1944, "Beauty of Chapel Hill is Monument to Coker," stated: "Dr. Coker has grown a great number of shrubs and trees which he has given away, both to the campus and to other private owners for the beautification of the town."[11]

In 1916, Coker was appointed to the Chapel Hill Board of Aldermen. He served on the town's tree committee and gave advice on downtown landscaping. Coker sought to protect the flora in the main commercial district of Chapel Hill, and at any threat to a planting of any sort, he sprang into action. Coker wrote to George Watts Hill, who also served on the Chapel Hill Tree Commission: "Some of these merchants over here, very shortsightedly in my opinion, seem to want to turn Chapel Hill into a place like any other little one-horse town trying to ape a city, and I think that you, and I, and everybody else who is familiar with the character and flavor and distinctive qualities of Chapel Hill ought to do everything we can to prevent such a thing."[12]

Coker was a caring, exceptional and popular teacher at the university, and he was a mentor for life to many students. He helped students with career plans and even assisted some with financial support. Twenty-five of his undergraduate students went on to earn master's degrees, nine doctoral degrees, and three were elected to the National Academy of Sciences. One of Coker's outstanding students was John Nathaniel Couch. In 1917, Couch was a third-year pre-med student at Trinity College (now Duke University). His training required a course in botany, which he opted to take at the University of North Car-

---

[10] "Botanist's Legacy," *Our Town, Chapel Hill News*, Sunday, February 23, 2003.
[11] Joslin, *Essays on William Chambers Coker*, 3.
[12] Ibid., 110.

olina at Chapel Hill. While there, he studied mycology with Dr. Coker. Couch soon abandoned his plans and became a student of botany at the university. Though his studies were interrupted by military service (World War I), he was eventually awarded three degrees in botany under the supervision of Coker. Coker remained a mentor and friend, and Couch went on to become a member of the National Academy of Sciences in 1943.

Another outstanding student was Alma Holland (Beers), who Coker hired as an undergraduate assistant in 1918, the first woman assistant in the Department of Botany at the university. She remained with the department for thirty-three years, contributing to the science of botany through research, teaching, and editing, and ensuring the smooth operation of the department. She provided significant assistance to Coker, typing his field notes, acquiring and curating botanical journals and books needed for research, mounting and classifying plant specimens, and much more. "Her contributions to botany were particularly significant when placed in the context of the time she lived."[13]

Exposure to Coker's teaching at the university, led another student, Paul W. Titman, who intended to major in art, to major in botany. The art department required students to take a class in botany. "I still remember," recalled Titman, "the first day of class, when a very distinguished, slim, elegant, white-haired, rosy-faced man, with a clipped white moustache came in and, in a deep South Carolina accent, introduced himself as William Chambers Coker. . . . I soon found that his approach to life mirrored my own aspirations. To put it into terms of my present perspective, he regarded botany as a humanity, a manifestation in the middle of all kinds of thought processes."[14] Coker encouraged his students to remain close to the natural world; he

---

[13] William R. Burk, "Alma Leonora Holland Beers: the First Woman Botanist at the University of North Carolina at Chapel Hill," *Journal of the North Carolina Academy of Science* 118, no. 4 (2002): 233.

[14] Joslin, *Essays on William Chambers Coker*, 120.

assigned field trips to study living plants and often went along. He supported practical experience and not just the reliance on book knowledge. He encouraged hard work and was not bound to his syllabus.

Coker also gave lectures and presentations world-wide on topics ranging from botany, science education, the philosophy of education, to the improvement of public grounds. He frequently received letters from public school officials and community leaders requesting his help for their schools. In this role and without pay, he traveled extensively throughout the state designing landscape plans for public schools. He was one of the first landscape advisors to school planners.

Over the years, many individuals at the university and in the community came to count on Dr. Coker to provide landscaping and gardening advice. This was the type of service that President Edward Kidder Graham considered not only essential for faculty to perform but also an important way for the university to give back to the larger community. Coker was well known throughout the Southeast, and residents would send him photographs of themselves standing with a tree or a shrub. Sometimes they simply wanted to share an unusual specimen; other times they asked for his help in identifying the specimen.

Coker was also associated with the Highlands Museum and Biological Laboratory in Highlands, North Carolina, known today as the Highlands Biological Station. He described the area around Highlands as the "biological crown of the southern Appalachians . . . and probably the richest biological area east of the Mississippi."[15] Research and teaching in herpetology, mycology, ornithology, ecology, and botany have continued to thrive at the Highlands Biological Station.

Preservation of unspoiled natural areas was Coker's passion. During the 1930s, he corresponded frequently with politicians

---

[15] Ibid., 69.

and foundations in Washington, DC, attempting to save the "primeval forest" near Highlands. He could be bold in expressing himself on social and political issues, and the university provided a climate to support this academic freedom. He endorsed the Versailles Treaty (in a letter to a French colleague) and worked against bans on the teaching of evolution. Coker joined fellow members of the North Carolina Academy of Science in opposing an anti-evolution bill in the North Carolina legislature, and he wrote supportively to a colleague in Oklahoma who had been fired for teaching evolution.

Among his other interests, Coker enjoyed writing poetry and short stories. One of Coker's ditties celebrated the 48th anniversary of two acquaintances, Mr. and Mrs. McIntosh, and ended with the lines, "what I call living, oh my gosh, wish I could live like a McIntosh." Coker's humor was known to be whimsical; he would chuckle and grin but seldom laugh out loud. Emily Guthrie, who spent months reviewing the collected papers of Dr. Coker, found a handwritten portion of a short story called "A Forest Love Story," which is peppered with plant puns—for example, "She murmured something in aloe voice."[16]

Coker desired to be surrounded by open land, like the environment from his childhood, and over time he became interested in purchasing real estate. In 1906, he bought farm land, considered then to be on the outskirts of Chapel Hill. For a time he devoted part of this land to farming. "In 1909, Coker built his home on part of the land, around towering specimen trees. He named the homestead, 'The Rocks,' after the dramatic outcropping of Chapel Hill granite. In 1944, Coker's property was described as seventy-five to eighty acres with a fine orchard of peaches, apples, pears and grapes."[17] As expected, he main-

---

[16] "Botanist's Legacy," *Our Town, Chapel Hill News*, Sunday, February 23, 2003.

[17] Joslin, *Essays on William Chambers Coker*, 6.

tained many well-cultivated gardens on this property. In the way that the university's arboretum demonstrated landscaping on a campus scale, Coker's garden at "The Rocks" modeled premier residential landscaping.

Coker was the original developer of Rocky Ridge Farm, now known as Laurel Hill. One of the earliest "planned" residential developments in North Carolina, it offered home sites near the campus, creating a community for faculty members and, at the same time, protecting and preserving the magnificent trees.

Beginning in 1924 and into the 1930s, Coker also made many land purchases in the Eastwood Lake area. These purchases, totaling approximately 230 acres, included land that would become part of today's Coker Hills. Some of the owners from whom Coker purchased properties, or who, at one point, had owned the land Coker bought, included J. Edward Clark, Jessie M. Henderson, O. B. Tenney, Newry Cole, S. M. Gattis, Jr., C. L. Lindsay, M. M. Durham, W. S. Crawford, Jr., Jack W. Sparrow, I. W. Prichard, and Robert L. Bynum.

Coker used the land he acquired for field trips with his students. In a letter to a professor at the University of Texas at Austin in 1919, Dr. Coker wrote about the characteristics of good teaching: "Do not be too bookish. Let the class collect their own material and take frequent excursions."[18]

In 1939-40, Coker hired R. M. Trimble to survey his many properties, including the Eastwood Lake properties, because there were some concerns about boundaries separating Coker's land from his neighbors' property. When Coker purchased land, zoning laws had not yet been passed by the town government. Coker would lay out large lots and place his own restrictive covenants in the deeds for these properties, limiting the number of structures allowed on each property, requiring quality construc-

---

[18] Ibid., 119.

tion, and barring buyers from raising cows and pigs on their property. He personally approved all the building plans on the properties he sold, until two years prior to his death.

William Chambers Coker's list of achievements is extensive. He pursued a demanding, diverse, and interesting life and remained a bachelor until his later years. In 1935, at age sixty-two, Coker married a lifetime friend thirteen years his junior, Louise Venable. Louise was the daughter of University of North Carolina at Chapel Hill President Frances Preston Venable. Like Coker, Louise was an avid gardener and was influential in Chapel Hill's garden club movement. She shared his interests and was a gracious host when friends came to visit. Several University of North Carolina at Chapel Hill scholarships and awards honor Louise and William Coker.

Coker was fond of dogs. As he turned seventy years old, his advice was, "marry the right woman and arrange to always have around a congenial dog."[19] His congenial dog, "Scott," accompanied him on his Sunday afternoon nature walks.

William Coker died in 1953, but his influence continues at the university, in Chapel Hill, and beyond. In celebration of the centennial of the Coker Arboretum, Professor Coker was remembered by his niece, Mary Coker Joslin, for "his devotion to science and the preservation of our natural heritage, his reverence for natural beauty, his gifts to his university and his state, his influence on his students, his many landscaping projects, and his practical ideals for education and its extension beyond academia. His productive life was that of a modest, hardworking, imaginative, humorous, kind, and generous man whose good taste and creative ideas remain alive today."[20]

In the Foreword of Joslin's book, *Essays on William Cham-*

---

[19] Ibid., 10.
[20] Ibid., 153.

bers Coker, Passionate Botanist*, the late University of North Carolina President Emeritus William C. Friday wrote: "In this time of hurried existence, let us heed the lessons exemplified by the life of this distinguished scholar, teacher, and good public servant. We will be better and much wiser citizens when we do."[21]

---

[21] *Ibid.*, xvi.

3//The Beginning of Coker Hills

My buildings will be my legacy . . . they will speak for me long after I'm gone. — Julia Morgan

When we build, let us think that we build forever. Let it not be for present delight nor for our use alone. Let it be such work as our descendants will look upon with praise and thanksgiving in their hearts. — John Ruskin

A love for the natural world, especially botany, was William Chambers Coker's daily inspiration and passion. Coker became fond of Chapel Hill as he discovered the region to be rich in botanical life. He immediately began work on researching the local flora and went on to publish a list of the woody plants he found in Chapel Hill. For Coker, the land deepened his interest in forests, woodlands and aging farmlands. For his students, land became the outdoor classroom and a living laboratory.

In a deed dated May 15, 1923, Coker sold and conveyed 43.5 acres of land to the Chapel Hill Country Club. The original country club was built along Country Club Road, near the University of North Carolina at Chapel Hill School of Law. When he acquired property, Coker anticipated some of his land would be "used as a wildlife refuge and as a location for botanical study."[1] Over time, he acquired hundreds of acres of land in Chapel Hill and elsewhere. In 1932, during the depths of the Depression, he purchased acreage to preserve the natural flora along the banks of Black Creek, west of Hartsville, South Carolina. This property is now part of Kalmia Gardens, the Botanical Garden at Coker

---

[1] *George Lee Simpson Jr., The Coker's of Carolina: A Social Biography of a Family (Chapel Hill: University of North Carolina Press, 1956), 245.*

College.

Coker bequeathed land to the University of North Carolina that became the display gardens of the North Carolina Botanical Garden and twenty-five acres of wooded terrain known as the Coker Pinetum. His other land holdings included acreage along Manning Drive, which was later purchased by the University. Coker's colleague and best friend, Dr. Henry Roland Totten, also became interested in real estate and worked as Coker's land agent for many years.

Not surprisingly, Chapel Hill was a very different community then. For example, the site of Eastgate Shopping Center was a vacant lot that could become a large pond during periods of heavy rain. When Eastgate was developed, it initially included an A&P Grocery Store, a hobby shop owned by Billy Arthur, a five and dime store, a bowling alley (where Trader Joe's is today), and an ABC (Alcohol Beverage Control) Liquor Store. The original ABC Store had a sales counter that ran the width of the store, limiting customer access to the products. Clerks provided customers with a list of available spirits, customers made their selections, and the clerks would bring the orders to the counter. The concept of self-service had not yet reached the ABC Store.

The present US Highway 15-501 had not yet been built, and the road to Durham was called Old Chapel Hill Road. On West Franklin Street, there was a Fowler's Grocery Store and a Belk's Department Store. Glen Lennox Shopping Center had a grocery market, and the Dairy Bar served sandwiches and ice cream. Popular restaurants included The Pines, The Ranch House, Brady's (known for their fried gizzards), and The Fish Camp in Carrboro. Restaurants in Orange County could not sell liquor, so patrons who wanted to drink spirits with their meals had to "brown bag"- bring their spirits wrapped in a brown paper bag.

Jack and Louise Behrman, early owners of property in

Coker Hills on Audubon Road, remembered an old barn and antique store that sat on the corner of East Franklin Street and South Elliott Road. They recalled attending a Chapel Hill dinner party, at which a friend asked if they had yet found property on which to build their new home. Louise excitedly responded, "Why yes, we just purchased two lots in Coker Hills." Their friend was stunned and, in a concerned voice replied, "My dear, if I was living in Coker Hills, I would feel like I was living way out in Durham."

In 1953, upon Coker's demise, his estate bequeathed many of his properties to Coker College. This was not surprising, since his family had been involved with the college since its founding. His father, James L. Coker, had created an endowment for the college, whose mission was to provide educational opportunities for women. Coker prepared the landscape design for the college and, in the late 1940s, donated funds for a new science building. He also encouraged some of his former graduate students to join the faculty at Coker College.

Coker College was well aware of the land development work done by Coker and Totten, and when the college began to consider developing some of the land in Chapel Hill from the Coker Estate, the college contacted Totten.

Henry Roland Totten was born in 1892, the son of William Theophilus and Jeannette Frances Barham Totten. He graduated from the Yadkin Collegiate Institute in 1909. He earned three degrees from the University of North Carolina at Chapel Hill, an A.B. degree in 1913, and an M.A. and Ph.D. in 1924. During World War I, Totten enlisted in the Reserve Officer Training Corps and became a Second lieutenant in 1917, serving in the field artillery in 1917 and 1918 and in France from 1918 to 1919. After WWI, he retained his army reserve commission, entering World War II as a Captain, and eventually rising to Lieutenant

Colonel. He married Addie Williams in 1923, and he returned to academics at the University as an assistant professor (1923–25), associate professor (1925–29), and full professor (1929–63). He retired from the University in 1963.

He was well-known for his work on the woody flora of the southeastern United States. His book on this topic, *Trees of the Southeastern States*, co-authored with Coker, is still considered an excellent guide to the trees of the region. Totten also authored a section on the *Fagaceae* (oak and beech tree family) for the *Manual of the Vascular Flora of the Carolinas*. A hybrid oak, *Quercus x totteni*, which grows near the front entrance of the Totten Center at the North Carolina Botanical Garden, was named in Totten's honor by Lionel Dane Melvin. Lionel Melvin was a well-known North Carolina nurseryman who promoted the use of native plants for landscapes. Melvin was also one of the founders of the North Carolina Wild Flower Preservation Society formed in 1951. Melvin and Totten formed a life-long friendship of scientific collaboration.

In 1944, when Coker retired, Totten replaced him as the new director of the Coker Arboretum. For many years, Coker and Totten proposed a more complete botanical garden than the Coker Arboretum, in a location south of campus. In 1952, seventy forested acres were dedicated for botanical garden development, the beginning of the North Carolina Botanical Garden. To this tract were added 103 acres of dramatic creek gorge and rhododendron bluffs, donated by William Lanier Hunt, a horticulturist and former student of Coker and Totten.

Like Coker, Totten loved to roam the fields and woods with his students, friends, and dogs. He was also a leader in wildflower preservation and influential in establishing garden clubs in North Carolina. He won numerous awards for teaching and for distinguished contributions to the training of students. The

Coker College Trustees doubted they could find a better individual to lead the development of the Coker Hills property.

From the earliest days of Coker Hills, Totten was instrumental in managing and supervising the design of the neighborhood. He initiated and attended meetings, managed inquiries, wrote letters and contractual agreements, approved invoices, spent long hours into the evening with contractors and weekends with potential buyers, stayed in constant communication with the Coker College Trustees, and advocated for the neighborhood to be named for his colleague and friend.

Totten accompanied prospective buyers to sites in Coker Hills, and he was known for his long strides as he walked with prospective buyers. Totten pointed out particular trees and told stories of the old logging trails and homesteads still evident in the woods. He explained how the Arrowwood viburnums found on many lots were so named because their straight stems were used by Native Americans for arrow shafts.

The Coker College Trustees along with Totten wished to see the neighborhood remain as a lasting legacy to William Chambers Coker. They believed the best way to do this would be to write a covenant describing the parameters for the neighborhood. A covenant is usually designed to protect a neighborhood's character and guide long-term development for an area. The covenant was given to each new owner and continued in perpetuity or to "run with the land." As homes were resold, the covenant was typically given to the buyer(s) at the time of the closing. Based on the terms of the Coker Hills covenant, decisions about building sites and house designs were approved by a majority vote of a five-person committee. "Those who served on the original committee included, Dr. Totten, W.H. Sory (Secretary of the Coker College Board of Trustees), Louise Venable Coker (Dr. Coker's widow), William Joslin (attorney and husband of Mary Coker Joslin), and R.G. Clawson (Treasurer of Coker College)."[2]

The Coker Hills Restrictive Covenant Agreement (Appendix 1) remains a registered document with the Clerk of Courts, Orange County, North Carolina.

Some years ago, the Town of Chapel Hill allowed neighborhoods, upon vote of the Town Council, to be designated as a Neighborhood Conservation District (NCD) (Appendix 2). Coker Hills received the NCD Designation that now serves as an overlay to the Town of Chapel Hill's R-1 zoning.

Totten's extensive correspondence and other documents provide a glimpse into the nature of his efforts during the development of Coker Hills. Based on these original documents, the following diary of the neighborhood development illustrates some of the challenges faced by Totten and the Coker College Trustees.

October 15, 1957: Totten to Dr. Whitehill, Faculty Member, Keio University, Tokyo

"We are having a very busy semester with a new Chancellor being installed and everyone is hard at work and seems reasonably happy. We attended the John Clayton (first botanist of Virginia) Day at Williamsburg. In addition to historical papers, there was an illustrated lecture by Lee Adams, an old student and assistant and a big exhibit of his flower paintings. I also had chats with other botanical friends of Virginia."

October 15, 1959: W.G. Fields, Jr., University Construction Company to Coker College

"This letter is in reference to your job in Chapel Hill on your property between Eastwood Lake and Estes Hills. After going over this work with your engineer, Mr. E.C. Leonard, we would like to quote our prices. . . . We can begin the work immediately to grade the street and

---

[2] H.R. Totten to William Joslin, January 7, 1965, Totten Papers, Box 11, Folder 135.

gravel, install concrete pipes, water lines, gate valves, water boxes, etc. in accordance with the University Water Department."

January 7, 1960: Fields to Coker College
"Installation of the water lines on the new graded street from Estes Hills School to Lakeshore Drive, Chapel Hill. Installation of the line will be in accordance with the University Water Department and will be under a 42 inch cover."

January 12, 1960: UNC Utilities Division to Totten
"This will confirm our recent conversation concerning the installation of water mains along the new road you have recently built between Estes Drive and Lakeshore Drive. We have agreed to install 2200 feet of pipe. The roadway must be dedicated for that use and accepted as part of the city or state system before we can begin work."

January 13, 1960:
"Mrs. Totten was in the Highsmith Hospital, Fayetteville, expected to be there for a while; she is in good spirits, progress good but is in a wheelchair."

January 21, 1960: Norman Baylor to Totten
"Relative to the joint venture of development of the area southwest of Lake Forest, formerly Eastwood Lake by the Coker Foundation and Mortgage Insurance Company as outlined in my letter of June 16, 1959. I wish to advise that the said work is nearly completed with the exception of laying the water line and paving the road. I understand I will be able to bill you for the Coker portion of the expense."

January 22, 1960: Totten to Mr. Sory, Secretary of Coker College
"Thanks for the promptness in getting an answer to the suggestions for naming Coker Hills Development and the roads."

February 19, 1960: Joseph Johnston, Secretary, Chapel Hill City Board of Education to Mr. Painter, State Highway
"The Chapel Hill City Board of Education is interested in the development of Curtis Road that will connect Estes Drive and the Lake Forest area. We are particularly interested in the development of this road because it will provide us with a most satisfactory access to our Estes Hills Elementary School. The Lake Forest area is in the Estes Hills Elementary School district. At the present time, it is necessary for those who live in Lake Forest and attend the Estes Hills School to travel Business Highway 501 in order to reach the school. The development of Curtis Road would simplify this problem and also make it possible for school authorities to render more satisfactory bus transportation. It is our understanding that the developer of this area, Coker College, has asked that Curtis Road be made a part of the state highway system. This letter is written in support of their application."

February 25, 1960: Totten to Mr. Sory
"I have enclosed two copies of the request for state maintenance of Clayton Road . . . I have had the forms for some time but wanted to get the complete backing of the Chapel Hill School Board. The Board has given their backing."

March 8, 1960: NC State Highway Commission to Totten
"Acknowledge your letter relative to the petition for addition of approximately 250 lin. ft. of Clayton Road and approximately 2,200 lin. ft. of Curtis Road located in Coker Hills. In order to expedite the addition of roads as requested it will be appreciated if you will furnish a copy of a plat indicating dedication of a 60-foot right of way for these roads. Also, please indicate if the plat has been recorded. We will be glad to further investigate these roads if you will advise when the work on the water lines, gas lines and graveling has been completed."

March 25, 1960: "Mrs. Totten home from the Highsmith Hospital."

April 14, 1960: Totten to Mr. Sory
"As for the Coker Hills section, they are now laying an 8-inch water line in Curtis Road; the gas people are laying the gas lines on the next

hill and will soon be to us. We are cutting the right of way to Clayton Road. This had to be done and to get it done now will simplify the survey work necessary for the sewer line in that section. . . . I shall send you soon a petition for signing to get the whole Coker Hills area changed from the present classification of Agricultural to R.A. 20. This should have been done before getting the preliminary approval of the roads and lots from the Planning Board and the Board of Aldermen but I overlooked it and so did they."

April 1960: Chapel Hill Board of Aldermen
"Approval given to rezone the Coker Hills land from Agricultural to R.A. 20 (the most restrictive zoning at that time for the Town of Chapel Hill)."

May 20, 1960: Totten to Mr. Sory
"As I reported yesterday by phone, the work on the roads in the Coker Hills Development is proceeding satisfactorily. Considerable grading has been done on Clayton Road and Elliott Road and some on Audubon Road. None of the culverts have been placed in the road and Mr. Fields of the University Construction Company says that he has to pay for the culverts. In other words, he would like a partial payment now. I have suggested that we pay him $5000 at this time. This would be about a third of the cost of the grading and graveling of 3,100 ft. of Elliott Road, 1,000 ft. of Clayton Road and 650 ft. of Audubon Road. I do not have an exact figure on the culverts. In any rate, considering the work that has already been done, $5000 is a reasonable payment and I do approve.
P.S. Please excuse the typing. I am trying to use my wife's portable and it is different from the one I usually work with."

June 15, 1960: Vernon Crook to Totten
"Since our conversation, I went to the Town Hall to take another look at the map of the Coker Hill's lots and road layout. You were gracious enough to ask if I was satisfied with the location of the proposed road that will provide access to my own land, and I assured you that I was. The road to my land is placed between Lots 47 and 48. Would it make a difference if it were moved over one lot and placed between lots 48 and 49?"

July 21, 1960: Totten to Mr. Sory
"Enclosed a statement from Mr. Leonard for the July work on the Coker Hills property. We are in the midst of examinations for the first term of Summer School, with notebooks, plant collections etc. to be checked out, so I have not had time to prepare the Realtor's Settlement Sheet, nor my own statement. . . . We have made real progress the last two weeks on Coker Hills and are now putting in water lines. Maybe if you could come up next week we could spend several hours checking what has been done, decide on several things, including restrictions and lot prices."

August 2, 1960: Totten to Mr. Sory
"If my addition is not in error again, the 61 lots we have listed would bring in $296,850. In addition, the three lots east of Velma Road were not counted in the above figures. I am discussing with one of the churches for all three lots on the north side of Elliott Road, not quite ready for listing, should bring in at least $45,000 and I think more with little additional expense. Six of the lots have been accepted at the prices offered. I have been out with others that I can expect to hear from in a few days."

August 5, 1960: Totten to Mr. Sory
"Since my letter of August 2, our offer of $6000 for Lot 64, corner of Michaux and Velma Road has been accepted and Lot 1, triangular lot at the western end of Curtis Road has tentatively been accepted for $4000. The State Road people have agreed to delay paving the section from the Durham Road to the Old Oxford Road; we have already paid the $500 as our part, long enough for us to put in the sewer line in that section if we move rapidly."

August 19, 1960: Totten to Mrs. Yohe, Rocky River, Ohio
"Thank you for your letter of August 12th. Considerable work has been done on the Coker Hills project, between the Estes Hills Development and the Lake Forest Development. The roads have been graded through most of the area that we plan to open up at this time and the water mains installed in them. Most of the roads will be curbed and guttered and most of them will be on sewer lines. It looks now that a

few will have to have septic tanks. Gas will be available and is already available for some lots. We have not yet presented the final plans to the Town Planning Board and Board of Aldermen, but our preliminary plans have been approved by both. We are now preparing a petition for the area to be brought into the town. This will take some time and we think now we can get it to them in October. However, we have ascertained starting prices and are now taking reservations on lots with prices from $4000–$6500. Of course, we can give no deed nor accept any payment at the present. When you are next in Chapel Hill, do give me the opportunity to show you the property."

August 30, 1960: Totten to Chapel Hill Board of Aldermen
"In April I presented the Coker College for Women of Hartsville, S.C. request that all of the Coker Hill property be rezoned from Agricultural to R.A. 20. This you approved. However, I find that in citing the boundaries of the property we unintentionally did not include a section of about 3.5 acres between the Old Oxford Road and the Chapel Hill-Durham Road . . . the part designated as Tract One and some pieces of property along the Lakeshore Drive, referred to as Tract Two in the petition. My statement to you in my letter of April 21 stated that the petition included the whole of the Coker Hills area. This was our intention. I trust that further action by you can correct any error. As a citizen of Chapel Hill who has worked for many years to help develop some of the finest residential parts of the town, I wish to point out that the Coker Hills area is one that the town can take real pride in-large lots that at a very early date will have very nice homes, much of the area with curb, gutter, pavement, gas and sewer lines. It adjoins the present town limits and should be in town. The Trustees of Coker College have gone to great expense in developing this area as a top residential property. In a way, it is a real monument, of more lasting value than the one in stone, to the late W.C. Coker, and through the names of its streets to southern botanists. Part of the undeveloped part is well suited to park purposes that will be needed in the future. Though it adds to the tax obligations of Coker College, as homes go up it will add to the tax revenue of Chapel Hill. Recognizing these things, Coker College, through its Board of Trustees, is petitioning that the whole area be incorporated into the town of Chapel Hill and hopes that this can be

done before any of the lots are sold, and that future wrangling between neighbors on that subject can be avoided."

September 1, 1960: Totten to Mr. Sory
"As per our telephone conversation last night, I enclose the suggested Restrictive Covenant Agreement for restrictions applicable to Coker Hills. If these are satisfactory, get them signed up and mail the original back to me for registering. However, feel free to make suggested changes. Also enclosed is the agreement to connect with the sewer. I got Mr. Leonard's statement for $490.63 for the period of August 16–31. Send the check to him directly for he will have to pay some of his help. Do come by the Suzanne Cottage [Totten's summer home in Myrtle Beach, SC]."

October 6, 1960: Totten to Mr. Sory
"The Chapel Hill Planning Board last night voted approval on the Section 1 of our Coker Hills. At the same time, we presented the nearly finished map of Section 2. It is so nearly completed that they approved that too, and we have completed the map. This means their chairman can sign it without bringing it to the whole board again. Their approval means we can take it to the Board of Aldermen next week. I hope that we can finish the second map by that time and get their approval for the two sections. After the Aldermen's approval, we have to register the completed maps in Hillsborough and can begin giving deeds. Twenty-one of our lots have now been spoken for. These twenty-one lots are valued at $100,200. I expect to have others by the end of the week. I enclose a statement from E.C. Leonard for engineering work for the Coker Hills section for the period of September 16–30th, inclusive for $297.15."

October 13, 1960: Ernest Hunt, UNC Class of 1934 to Totten
"My uncle, Ben Fountain, informed me you were handling the disposal of lots in the new development known as Coker Hills in Chapel Hill. In all the time I have been away from Chapel Hill since graduation . . . I have looked forward to returning to Chapel Hill to make it my home at some future date. Uncle Ben said that he and Dr. Ben Fountain Jr. purchased a lot in Coker Hills. . . . I would be very happy to purchase a lot on either side of the two lots. My wife is the former Mary King

Fountain of Fountain, NC. I am enclosing my check in the amount of $225 as a 5% binder of Good Faith indication."

October 16, 1960: Totten to Mr. Sory
"I have agreed to hold off the market the three lots at the east end of the property that would make such a nice church site until December 15, asking price $15,000. The Presbyterian Church is looking for a site for a second church for the future. This site is ideal for them, but like the University, there is a lot of red tape and approvals that are needed. . . . We have been making slow progress on the sewer line for we have been running into rock, but hope to move faster soon."

October 19, 1960: Totten to Hunt
"I have received your letter and check for a lot in Coker Hills. By my returning your check, please do not get the idea that we do not want you in the Coker Hills development. For we are looking forward to having you as a citizen of Chapel Hill and in the Coker Hills part of town. I prefer not to sell the property, sight unseen. We have a variety of lots in the development and we are planning to add more at an early date. I like to go over the possibilities with the would-be purchaser and if possible for his wife to see the property too and I can go over our plans for the area."

October 28, 1960: Totten to Dr. James Masson, Chemstrand Corporation
"I enclose a rough sketch of your lot and the surrounding lots. If this is not sufficient, please let me know. I am also enclosing a copy of the restrictions that apply to the Coker Hills area."

October 30, 1960: Totten to Mr. Sory
"I enclose two copies of the Restrictive Agreement for Coker Hills and a bill for $6 from the Bowman Typing Service for 100 mimeographed copies of the same. I am also enclosing the tax bill for 1960. It seems this should include taxes for all the real estate owned by Coker College within town during 1960."

November 4, 1960: Totten to Mr. Sory
"This morning Mr. Leonard and I have gone over the ground with the power line folks and have agreed with them on the placement of the power poles over most of the area, including the area for which power will be needed very soon. . . . I expect this work to be done next week."

November 8, 1960: Hunt to Totten
"I wish to acknowledge with thanks your letter enclosing a copy of the restrictions regarding Coker Hills. I wish to say that both Mrs. Hunt and I have a great appreciation for these restrictions that have been registered on the Public Records of Orange County and feel that persons of wonderful judgment and great foresight must have crafted the same. We will be running a rather tight schedule from the time we leave Daytona Beach . . . for Atlanta . . . we have reservations at the University Motel . . ."

November 11, 1960: Totten to Hunt
"Thank you for your letter with your plans to visit Chapel Hill. I have a class that morning but can meet you later in the day. Parking is more of a problem on campus now than when you were a student. Perhaps I can arrange to pick you up at the hotel. . . . As to the payment, we are trying to keep our sales on a cash basis. I am my whole office force, with most of my real estate business for Coker College. Before Dr. Coker's death, I handled most of his land sales work, and supervised the planning of the lots. Through the years we built a reputation for fair dealing and getting done what we promised to do and seeing that restrictions were lived up to. One of the things we tried to do, not always successfully, was to keep our lots out of the hands of speculators and in so doing try to hold prices down to reasonable figures and our bills were paid so promptly that construction bids were low. My other job was to place people on land that they liked and appreciated. . . . Dr. Coker left most of his real estate around Chapel Hill to the Coker College, founded by his father and to which Dr. Coker for years had been a heavy contributor and advisor. The Trustees of Coker College seem to have liked the way we had been developing land here and asked me to carry on. I work very closely with the Secretary of the Board of Trustees. You can see why keeping this as simple as possible under our set

up works best."

November 13, 1960: Totten to Dr. Howard Clark
"I have enclosed the Realtor's Settlement Sheet. . . . As you know the grading work on the roads in this section has been completed, the water lines are in, and work is proceeding on the sewer line and the power line. We hope to get the curb and gutter work started next week. The gas people have been waiting for us to complete the excavation work for the sewer lines before they install the gas line."

November 20, 1960: Totten to Dr. Patrick Hobson
"Enclosed is the Realtors Settlement Sheet, as you know the grading work on the roads in this section has been done, the water lines are in, work on the sewer lines and power lines is progressing. We expect to start work on the curbs and gutters very soon but the paving work may have to wait until the spring or summer."

November 24, 1960: Totten to Mr. and Mrs. Barton
"The water lines in both streets, Michaux and Velma Road, have been installed; the sewer lines and power lines are now being built. The curb and gutter work has been started in the development, and we plan to reach your two roads at an early date. However, to date we have not been able to get the cooperation of the owners of the land on the south side of Velma Road, and it may be impossible to get the curb and gutter on their side of the road. The surfacing may have to wait until spring or next summer, but the black top surfacing of regular width will be made by Coker College. There is ample room in the right of way of both roads for future sidewalks, but Coker College does not obligate itself for the building of the sidewalks."

November 24, 1960: Totten to Mr. Sory
"In reference to the work on Velma Road, I had a long conference last night with Grady Pritchard and Mr. Leonard. Grady and I requested a map from Mr. Leonard showing the small tracts that we need deeds for. Grady is not ready to develop his land south of Velma Road." [Some of this property eventually became the Chapel Hill Public Library/Pritchard Park.]

December 3, 1960: E.C. Leonard to Mr. Sory
(handwritten letter)

"As you may recall the matter came up in regard to a building lot in Coker Hills for us. During the conversation something was said, that if we paid for the curb and gutter, hard surfacing and the proportional part of the sewer, under these conditions you would consider giving us the lot. We would like to hear from you as soon as possible as we have to make some definite plans as to our future home. The curb and gutter are coming along fine; the biggest worry of course is the sewer line along the Durham Highway. We have the promise of a second machine to start digging at the other end. The house on Lot 41 has been started and a lot on Clayton is being cleared for building. The Hobson and Carter houses have been put up for bid."

December 6, 1960: Mr. Sory to E.C. Leonard

"I have been impressed with your good work on Coker Hills and appreciate your loyalty and good will toward our entire project. To show this appreciation for what you have done and to insure your continued support and to have you living in the midst of the project, it was my idea to give you the lot of your choice and have you pay only for the cost of the services, water sewer, curb, gutter and blacktop. In the case of the water and sewer, you would pay half and the owner on the other side would be considered to have half assessed. If you are ready to get started, I will have Dr. Totten get the deed prepared. All good wishes."

December 16, 1960: Totten to Mr. and Mrs. Whitfield, High Point, NC

"I did discuss your case with Coker College, and we wish to continue the development on a cash basis. I have no office help here and Hartsville is a considerable distance away. They would prefer to keep my time for the planning, supervising and selling part rather than collecting. There are a number of lending agencies that would be glad to help you. I am still holding both lots for you, Lot 54 on Velma with the view and Lot 56 on Michaux Road . . . I cannot hold these lots for long. Our expenses are mounting up considerably faster than we expected and the unspoken lots have advanced in price. I could hold the lots for a week or more if we find it necessary. Lot 54 has the better view and has about .7 acreage. The other lot has slightly more than an acre. We do want you in Coker Hills and I wish to be of help."

January 19, 1961: Totten to Mr. Sory
"The Chairman of the Committee for the selection of a church site for a second Presbyterian church has told me that our site has been selected."

January 23, 1961: Totten to Mr. Sory
"The roads in the area following the installation of sewer lines, curb and gutters, rains and freezes are in a sad state. I have put on a good layer of gravel. With so many houses now building, I must keep the roads passable. My fear now is that some of the houses will be ready for occupancy before that main sewer line on the highway is completed. Fields still thinks that he can complete that line with a month of good weather but I don't think we can expect a month of good weather in the immediate future. He is having a tough time of it on the sewer line and is using very expensive machinery for that work. I know that I have to be sure... that he does not fail. He is doing a good although slow job . . ."

January 25, 1961: Mr. Sory to HR Totten
"Confidential and not to be discussed, I find that a big newsbreak is to come about the Triangle. It says that GE is to come in with a sizeable set up that means more people who will want lots. It may mean that demand will be good enough we can boost our prices a little."

February 4, 1961: Totten to Mr. Sory
"I enclose a statement from E. C. Leonard for $281.75 for Engineering Services in the Coker Hills area for January 16–31. Wednesday evening I attended a public hearing on the long range planning for the roads in and around Chapel Hill and Carrboro. As you know, I have been worried all along of the rumored possibility of a by-pass road right through Coker Hills, but the planners have taken consideration of the first class residential development we have already developed there and our future plans. I am so glad that we had not delayed any longer in getting a real start. I feel that we are now safe on that score. Nevertheless, I plan to attend meetings of the Planning Board and Board of Aldermen's

meeting where final approval of Plans is expected. I think they come up next week, at least one of them. We are having real winter now. I hope that you and Mrs. Sory are enjoying fine weather in Florida."

February 6, 1961: Totten to Mr. William Joslin, Coker College Trustee

"I am enclosing building plans for the home of Dr. Howard Clark, of the Chemstrand Corporation for Lot 36, Section 1, and Sheet 1 of Coker Hills. As you know three of the five (Secretary of the Board, Mr. Story; Treasurer of the College, Mr. Clawson; Mr. Joslin, Mrs. Louise Coker, and H.R. Totten) have to approve the exterior lines and placement on the lot. Several houses are now going up, approved by Mrs. Coker, Mr. Sory, and H.R.T., and when I had the three signatures for approval, I had not bothered the other two. However, Mr. Sory planned to leave today on a trip to Florida and will be out of Hartsville until the 17th. So I am sending this one on to you. If you could approve and sign, send it back to me. The severe winter weather has held up our construction work on curbs, gutters, sewer lines, etc. but when better weather returns we will move right ahead."

February 15, 1961: Totten to Mr. Sory

"The plans for the Clark lot were approved including approval by Mrs. Coker. By the way, Dr. Clark is at present first man in a big research section of Chemstrand . . . and will have a big laboratory and a lot of new men to come in yet. We should be able to furnish lots to a lot of them. We have had a few good days and are making progress on that sewer line. It is time for one or two of the new houses to be ready for occupancy in about two weeks. The roads are in terrible shape, but with one or two more drying days, we should be able to start graveling. I believe I have a better solution for the Lots 26, 27 and 28. Lot 28 has to be enlarged to bring it up to .6-acre minimum. I am holding the deed for the lot prepared on the original survey and the purchaser has the money ready, but it will require a new map and a new deed. The plan I outlined to you was to combine Lot 26 with the remains of Lot 27 into one lot. However, I have gone over the ground again and now believe that a better solution would be to enlarge the remainder of Lot 27 with enough of Lot 26 to bring Lot 27 up to standard and then to give the rest of Lot 26 to the Town for a small playground of about ½ acre. It would add little to the sale value of Lot 27 to add all of Lot 26 to it and I am afraid it would remain a low blackberry, honeysuckle jungle eyesore for the neighborhood. Soon all the new developments will have to set aside certain areas for playgrounds and we will get good publicity and goodwill by leading rather than to be forced to do it. We will soon be finishing that sewer line, and I still have hopes of getting some help on it."

February 22, 1961: Totten to Mr. Sory
"I have enclosed a statement from Purser and London, Inc. for the sewer pump that shall be installed at the intersection of Clayton and Audubon Roads. I believe we got the best terms possible by ordering from the Town Manager. This will be installed under the supervision of the Town authorities. I have also enclosed a statement from E.C. Leonard for $217 for highway sewer and storm sewer engineering and supervision for Jan. 16–31, 1961. When the weather gets more favorable, we will be able to move along faster with that end of the work. I have received from Joslin the approval of the Clark house. Reservations are made for you and Mrs. Sory at the University Motel for Tuesday night, Feb. 28th. I believe I told you I was leaving for a short trip to Highlands on March 10th."

March 17, 1961: Totten to Mr. Sory
"I enclose the building plans for Dr. and Mrs. Barton, Lot 55 corner of Michaux and Velma Road. I have written my approval and have forwarded it on to the Hartsville folks . . . the title is being worked on for the church property. I expect to get the Pritchard's signatures on the deed for the small tract we are exchanging with them, also their signature for the dedication paper for Velma Road. The drying weather is allowing much better progress on our roads."

March 23, 1961: Totten to Mr. Sory
"Rain has held up that sewer line on the highway. I have not been out there this morning, but hope that dirt and rock are moving again."

March 23, 1961: Totten to Mr. and Mrs. Clements
"Your lot should be designated in the directory listings as 1603 Curtis Road. We do not know when mail delivery will start for that section but when a few more homes have been built, all of us should urge the Post Office for an early start."

April 15, 1961: Mr. Sory to Totten
"It was a pleasure to get your recent letters with checks and deeds. You will be pleased to see from the memo I am enclosing that we are in the red just about $17,000. These figures come from my records. I want to congratulate you on the fine job you have done. I often wonder how we could have made out without Mr. Leonard. He has done a fine job and never stops. I wonder about the house situation, I have seen no deed for the lot we gave him."

April 17, 1961: Totten to Mr. Sory
"Your estimate of Mr. Leonard is correct. He has just been too busy to get the surveying done for his lot, which is necessary before we can draw up the deed."

April 28, 1961: Totten to Rev. Thrasher
"The sewer line, curb and gutter, gravel and most of the storm sewers are in on Wood Circle and Elliott Road. The sewer line should be in working order in a few days for we are nearly through the work on the Chapel Hill-Durham Highway. We plan to surface these roads this summer."

April 28, 1961: S. A. White Furniture Company, Mebane, NC, to Totten
"Mrs. White and I have signed codicils to our wills leaving to the church any of this Coker property which we might still own in case we should both die before our gifts to the church were made."

May 13, 1961: Totten to Mr. Sory
"I had hoped to report the laying of the last piece of sewer pipe along the Highway in this letter. At 2:30 yesterday afternoon only three pieces were left but by 3 pm the rains really came down and they had

to give up. There is still some testing, inspecting, back filling, leveling of shoulders etc. to be done."

May 16, 1961: Totten to Mr. Sory
"As mentioned earlier, Lot 28 did not quite measure up to the .6 acre and a part had to be taken from the old No. 27, then a part from Lot 26. Lot 26 is not a suitable building lot anyway, and we have agreed to turn it over to the Town for a playground. The sewer line along the Highway seems to be ready for sewage and we are making good progress on the part of the sewer line not completed on Clayton Road."

May 17, 1961: Totten to Mr. Sory
"The sewer line along the Highway seems to be ready for sewage as soon as we can get the Town sanitary inspector to check it. We hope to get this done today, but it may be tomorrow. There is considerable dressing up to be done along the right of way, but it was so muddy this morning that we postponed that for some drying out and hope to do that tomorrow."

June 28, 1961: Totten to Dr. Wilcox
"We are about ready to start paving the roads in Coker Hills and we hope to get the connections from the sewer and water mains from the trunk lines to the property lines before the pavement is laid."

August 5, 1961: Totten to Mr. Sory
"I left with eleven graduate students for our mountain trip and returned yesterday. We had a good trip. I was out inspecting the work done in my absence with Mr. Leonard. Considerable progress has been made but two days of rain slowed things up. Some work is going on with catch basins and smoothing up the roads. The Rev. Thrasher's plans for his house on Wood Circle were not quite ready when I left. He was trying to get away for his vacation."

August 12, 1961: Totten to Mr. Sory
"I am leaving with my Dendrology class Monday for a study of the woody plants of the coastal plain and seashore. Enclosed are copies of the settlement sheets for the Yohe and Tenney sales."

August 26, 1961: Totten to Mr. Sory
"While visiting a niece out of state, Addie fell last Sunday and broke both bones in her right leg below the knee, very close to the break made when hit by an automobile in 1959. She was able to come in by plane but is now in the hospital. She is in good spirits and if phlebitis does not set in as before, she will make it."

September 11, 1961: Totten to Mr. Sory
"I have enclosed a check from Charles Hinsdale for his lot. This afternoon, they told me the pouring and packing of the blacktop should start tomorrow. I have made a reservation for you at the Carolina Inn for your visit. I think you will find Coker Hills looking mighty good by that time."

December 8, 1961: Totten to Mr. Sory
"This week we continued clean up jobs, grading sidewalks and sowing grass. The development really looks good and will really look good after the next rain."

January 23, 1962: Ben Fountain to Totten
"Enclosed is the check to cover the cost for the apron on 400 Clayton Road. We are very happy in Elizabeth City although we miss Chapel Hill a great deal. We drive through Coker Hills every month or so and it does look beautiful. You should be very proud of it. The area is a credit to Chapel Hill and the State."

February 15, 1962: Totten to Mr. Sory
"We have now had three fine spring days and the grass along our roads is beginning to really show."

February 22, 1962: Totten to Mr. Sory
"My last letter to you I mentioned the threat of a lien on Coker Hills and hoped it could be avoided. Fields delivered a check to the Chatham Brick and Tile Company and brought a receipt back but, as I feared, the check 'bounced'. The Brick Company has instructed their attorney to place the lien not on the whole development but only on one lot. We have chosen Lot 65 . . . I tried to persuade them to hold off the lien to

give Mr. Fields every chance to raise the money. With the check bouncing there was nothing else to do. We find that he owes another man about $1200 for gravel delivered to Coker Hills. That too will probably mean another lien. I am terribly disappointed, but much relieved we can still give good titles for the other lots."

February 27, 1962: W. Marshall Smith, Attorney to Coker College
"This is to notify you that the lien against one of the Coker Hills lots has now been cancelled. Thank you for your cooperation."

March 21, 1962: Mrs. Bunn to Totten
"After consideration of the restrictive covenant, we do wish to purchase and build on the Michaux lot. We appreciate your kindness to us last Saturday."

April 26, 1962: Totten to Mrs. Bunn
"There are now nine houses going up in the development and I am expecting another one to start next week."

February 4, 1965: Totten to Mr. Sory
"Plans for Dr. and Mrs. Dearborn's Lot 74. Mrs. Coker left a few days ago for a cruise for a month or more, so did not get to show her the plans. In my opinion, the house will look good on the lot."

March 12, 1965: Totten to Mr. Sory
"Curtis Road for a long time was a source of irritation. For the Lake Forest people it cut off about a mile to the Estes Hills School. At that time, the Lake Forest people would do nothing toward getting the sewer line in, and we could not develop that area without sewer. Lake Forest was not in the Town and could not get in until they had raised their standards as to the sewers, curb, and gutters. Finally, Mr. Owens bought up the undeveloped part of Lake Forest. He lives there himself. He offered to pay in part the costs of shaping up and graveling the road and so making it a good base when the sewer line did come. Finally, the sewer arrangement with the town was agreed upon and the Town accepted most of Lake Forest."

September 9, 1968: Totten to Mr. Clawson, Treasurer of Coker College

"Mr. Thrasher, the Episcopal minister whose home was on Lot 59 Wood Circle, died a few months ago. The home was bought by Mr. R.J. Myers. He wishes to add a garage to the house and has submitted the enclosed plans. I have gone over the plans with him and looked over the lot again. I find nothing in the plans that would conflict with our restrictions and recommend that we approve."

April 1969: Town Appearance Commission to Totten

"We all express our appreciation for the splendid street tree survey. We realize it is not complete but hope you will continue to work on it, advising the town on street matters. The map will surely serve as a handy reference to tree location, species, condition, problems, age- thank you for the many hours and energy you have given this project and which will serve as a reminder of your dedication to trees."

December 3, 1970: Totten to Clawson

"I enclose plans for a house on Lot 1 in Coker Hills. It's a rather difficult lot and I think the plans shown will be as good as one can expect of the lot. As usual in such cases, they hope to get building right away."

April 27, 1970: Totten to Mr. Clawson

"Enclosing building plans for a house on Lot 4, owned by Mr. and Mrs. Rupert Hanny, the former Mrs. M.F. Townend, who bought two large Lots 3 and 4. The plans here submitted will not increase the number of houses allowed for the two, but does require a change in the line between the two. This is allowable as each new lot will be large enough for our restrictions. The new house will be nearer the road but still 50' from the road. This will not be near Lot 5 owned by Dr. Stehman. They originally bought two lots, built on Lot 6, then were moved to New York and sold the house they built, but kept Lot 5 to build on latter. Coker College and I approve the house position."

February 2, 1971: Totten to National Institute for Real Estate Brokers

"Although my state license as a Real Estate Broker is paid through June 1971, I have retired from the Chapel Hill Board of Realtors. At age 78, retirement is desirable. "

September 15, 1972: Totten to Clawson
"I enclose plans for the residence of Mr. and Mrs. Sears for Lot 130. I received the plans yesterday and went out with Mr. David Curl of Orange Builders to look over the lot and plans. The lot is a difficult one, a steep hillside. They are trying to save the desirable trees and are abiding by the restrictions. The Orange Builders have built several nice homes in the area and they are trying to fit the house to the lot. I recommend approval."

Naming of the Streets

Have you ever wondered how a street got its name? "Main" Street is usually obvious, and if you are driving in Washington, DC, many of the streets are named for states in the union. William Penn, a nature-lover, had his hand in naming many of Philadelphia's streets for trees and plants, like Vine, Chestnut, and Filbert.

A casual perusal of the street names in Coker Hills makes one wonder about the rationale behind the names Totten selected for this development. But upon reflection, the fact that Coker and Totten were both southern botanists provides a clue to the commonality among the honored individuals. In fact, Coker Hills may be the only neighborhood in the country with streets named for southern botanists/naturalists.

Coker and Totten greatly appreciated the pioneering work of those whose names appear on our street signs. For instance, Elliott was called the "father of southern botany," Clayton was a colonial botanist, Curtis was a pioneer in the field of mycology, and Michaux was held in high esteem for his pioneering work and interest in the botany of the south.

The following section provides a brief biography for each of the nine honorees. Unlike William Penn, who demonstrated his love of nature by naming streets for botanical species, it is interesting that Dr. Totten selected botanists for this enduring honor.

Allard Road

Harry Ardell Allard*
1880-1963

Harry Allard, originally from Oxford, Massachusetts, graduated from the University of North Carolina in 1905. He was eight years younger than Coker and stayed on as a botany laboratory assistant in Coker's research lab after his graduation. Allard remained in that position for a year, helping with plantings in the Coker Arboretum and the completion of many ink drawings of plants. There was a lifelong admiration between Coker and Allard. Allard named his second son, William Coker, but sadly, the 1923 edition of the UNC General Alumni class notes reported that Allard's son died when he was only three months old.

Allard, who Coker considered to be one of his best students, went on to study ways to improve plants and planting methods with the Federal Bureau of Plant Industry in Washington, D.C., now known as the U.S. Department of Agriculture. "He is perhaps best known as the co-discoverer of floral photoperiodism."[3] Many flowering plants use a photoreceptor protein to sense seasonal changes in night length or photoperiod, which

---

Photo courtesy of the Hunt Institute for Botanical Documentation, Carnegie Mellon University, Pittsburgh, Pa.

[3] *Mary Coker Joslin, Essays on William Chambers Coker, Passionate Botanist (Chapel Hill: University of North Carolina at Chapel Hill Library, 2003), 122.*

they use as signals to flower. "In 1920, W.W. Garner and H.A. Allard published their discoveries on photoperiodism and felt it was the length of daylight that was critical."[4]

Two years after Allard's retirement from government service, the University of North Carolina at Chapel Hill awarded him an honorary degree (Doctor of Science). The following tribute to Allard was read at that ceremony:

"Harry Ardell Allard, B.S., North Carolina, 1905, where he worked his way through college; W.C. Coker's first laboratory assistant; helped in the first plantings in the now famous Coker Arboretum, worked under Dr. H. J. Weber in the U.S. Department of Agriculture in the breeding of corn, cotton, pineapples, sorghum and broom corn hybrids. His original research in tobacco induced a new outlook and interest in virus diseases; his work in the photoperiodic behavior of plants became a turning point in the understanding of plant growth and reproduction as influenced by seasons and climate conditions in all parts of the world; author of 300 scientific papers largely dealing with the ecology of plants and the stridulations of insects. A naturalist who loves plants, people, and life anywhere, one of those pioneer scientists who in the quiet of nature's laboratories, blazes modestly the trails that become the highways of the world's life. By vote of the Faculty and Trustees of the University of North Carolina, we confer upon you the degree of Doctor of Science."[5]

---

[4] Capon, Brian. *Botany for Gardeners* (2nd. ed.). (Portland, OR: Timber Publishing, 2005). 148.
[5] *Joslin, op. cit.*, p. 122.

Audubon Road

John James Audubon*
1785–1851

One of the most famous 19th-century American ornithologists and naturalists, Audubon is best known for his beautiful watercolors of birds and plants. He was born on the island of San Dominque in 1785. His father was a French merchant and his mother, who died when he was a child, was a Creole chambermaid from Louisiana. His father owned a plantation in America and aided Americans during the American Revolution. In 1803, Audubon decided to come to the United States to manage his father's plantation and to escape Napoleon's military draft. On the voyage to America, he changed his name from Jean Jacques Fougere Audubon to John James Audubon. Between 1808 and 1820, he frequently changed occupations as he followed his passion to explore the wilderness and sketch birds and plants. Unable to financially support his family with his wildlife paintings, he began to paint portraits for a livelihood. Audubon was a self-taught artist and scientist. In 1830, he was elected as a Fellow to the American Academy of Arts and Science. His well-known publication, *Birds of America*, was followed by a sequel,

---

*Photo courtesy of the Hunt Institute for Botanical Documentation, Carnegie Mellon University, Pittsburgh, Pa.

Ornithological Biographies.

During the 1830s, Audubon continued to make expeditions in North America. During a trip to Key West, Florida, a companion wrote in a newspaper article, "Mr. Audubon is the most enthusiastic and indefatigable man I ever knew... Mr. Audubon was nether dispirited by heat, fatigue, or bad luck... he rose every morning at 3 o'clock and went out... until 1 o'clock. Then he would draw the rest of the day before returning to the field in the evening, a routine he kept up for weeks and months."[6]

Clayton Road

Claytonia virginica*
John Clayton
1694–1773

John Clayton, a colonial plant collector, is considered the first botanist of Virginia. He was born in England and moved to Virginia with his father in 1715. He lived near the Chesapeake Bay and actively explored the botany of the region. Clayton's name first appeared in colonial records in 1720 as the Gloucester County Clerk. He held this position for more than fifty years recording deeds, land surveys, and other official documents.

Clayton owned a tobacco plantation but devoted much of his time to the study of botany. By 1735, he was regularly providing

---

[6] Rhodes, Richard. *John James Audubon: The Making of an American*, New York: Alfred A. Knopf, 2004, p.366.
*Courtesy Alan Cressler, Lady Bird Johnson Wildflower Center

naturalists such as Mark Catesby and John Frederick Gronovius with botanical specimens to be identified. Among other accomplishments, he named the *genus Agastache*, a group of perennial flowering herbs. In 1737, Swedish botanist Carolus Linnaeus named a genus of wildflowers, *Claytonia*, in Clayton's honor. Clayton compiled for Gronovius, a catalog of herbs, fruits and trees, all native to Virginia. Gronovius translated this catalogue into Latin and published it as *Flora Virginica* (1739) without Clayton's permission. This publication and later editions were the earliest efforts to identify the native botanical species of the South. Until the mid-twentieth century, this was the only publication on the native plants of Virginia. By 1740, Clayton began corresponding with the leading Pennsylvania botanist, John Bartram. This correspondence and the ensuing exchange of seeds and advice lasted for several decades. Bartram described Clayton as a "worthy, ingenious man" and his garden as the best he had ever seen in Virginia.

In 1794, Sir Joseph Banks acquired the specimens Clayton originally sent to Gronovius, and these now comprise a collection known as the John Clayton Herbarium at the Natural History Museum in London. There are no known images of Clayton, and many of his records and papers were likely destroyed by a fire in the clerk's office in New Kent County, Virginia, where the papers were being stored. Virginia continues to hold John Clayton in high esteem and sponsors "John Clayton Day" in Williamsburg, Virginia. The John Clayton Chapter of the Virginia Native Plant Society, an organization founded in 1984, is named in honor of this colonial botanist.

Curtis Road

Moses Ashley Curtis*
1808–1872

Moses Ashley Curtis, Episcopal pastor and Carolina botanist, was born on May 11, 1808, in Stockbridge, Massachusetts. He attended Stockbridge Academy and graduated from Williams College in 1827. After graduation, he left New England for Wilmington, North Carolina, where he served as a tutor for the family of North Carolina Governor Edward Bishop Dudley and began studying local plants. Curtis returned to Massachusetts in 1833 to study for the ministry under the Church of the Advent. On December 3, 1834, he married Mary De Rosset of Wilmington, North Carolina. The following year he was ordained.

Reverend Curtis began his ministry as a missionary in western North Carolina, serving congregations in Lincolnton, Salisbury, Morganton, and Charlotte. From 1837 to 1839, he taught at the Episcopal School in Raleigh, North Carolina, the predecessor to St. Mary's College. He was called back into the mission field in 1840 to Washington, North Carolina. After serving there for a year, he accepted a call to St. Matthew's Episcopal Church in Hillsborough, North Carolina, where he remained for the rest of his life, with the exception of the years of 1847-1856, when he

---

*Photo courtesy of the Hunt Institute for Botanical Documentation, Carnegie Mellon University, Pittsburgh, Pa.

was in charge of a parish at Society Hill, South Carolina (home of Dr. Coker's grandparents). In addition to being a minister and a botanist, Curtis was a talented musician who played several instruments, including the piano, organ, flute, and violin. He also composed anthems and hymns, such as "How Beautiful upon the Mountain."

Curtis, a dedicated pastor, was also known for his accomplishments in botany, especially his work in mycology-the study of fungi. Prior to his contributions, the study of fungi had been limited. Curtis discovered forty different species of mushrooms within two miles of his home. He believed the food shortages that haunted the southern armies during the Civil War would not have been as severe had there been better knowledge of edible fungi. To that end, Curtis used himself as a food taster/tester for each of the mushroom species he identified. "As a botanist, Curtis explored the southern Appalachian Mountains, embarking on a major expedition in 1839. He maintained a herbarium of dried specimens and contributed specimens to John Torrey and Asa Gray. He collected lichens for Edward Tuckerman and corresponded with many other botanists, including mycologist Miles Joseph Berkeley to whom he sent many specimens with descriptions and notes. Gray said of him that "No living botanist...is so well acquainted with the vegetation of the southern Allegheny Mountains..." and that he "...was among the first to retrace the steps and rediscover the plants found and published by the elder Michaux, in the higher Allegheny Mountains."[7]

One of his most recognized published works is his 1860 *Geological and Natural History Survey of North America, Part III, Botany*. Moses Ashley Curtis died on April 10, 1872 and was buried at St. Matthew's Episcopal Church in Hillsborough, North Carolina. A highway marker commemorating his life is

---

[7] Wikipedia contributors. Moses Ashley Curtis (botanist). Wikipedia, The Free Encyclopedia. 20 July 2016. Web. 25 July 2016.

located on US 70 Business, Churton Street, near St. Matthew's Episcopal Church in Hillsborough, North Carolina.

Elliot Road

Stephen Elliot*
1771–1830

Stephen Elliott was born in Beaufort, South Carolina, on November 11, 1771. He attended Yale College (now University) and graduated as class valedictorian in 1791. "He was elected to the South Carolina State Legislature in 1793 or 1796 (sources disagree) and served until the turn of the century. He was then re-elected to the legislature in 1808, and in that role worked toward the establishment of a state central bank. When the bank was founded in 1812, he resigned from the legislature and was appointed president of the Bank of the State of South Carolina."[8]

Elliott's leisure time was devoted to literature and science, and he pursued his study of botany with enthusiasm. In 1813, he was instrumental in founding the Literary and Philosophical

---

*Photo courtesy of the Hunt Institute for Botanical Documentation, Carnegie Mellon University, Pittsburgh, Pa.

[8] *Wikipedia contributors. Stephen Elliott (botanist). Wikipedia, The Free Encyclopedia. 20 July 2016. Web. 25 July 2016.*

Society of South Carolina, serving as the group's first president. He lectured on botany without pay and was for some time editor of the *Southern Review*. In 1825, he helped to establish the Medical College of South Carolina, where he was appointed as a professor of natural history and botany. He held this position until his death in 1830.

The material that Elliott collected on numerous field trips and his intimate knowledge of the southeastern flora was of great value to other botanists. Elliott's herbarium was one of the largest in America, and the specimens proved valuable to John Torrey, Asa Gray, and others. Today, Elliott's herbarium is found in the Charleston Museum, Charleston, South Carolina. His classic work, *A Sketch of the Botany of South Carolina and Georgia*, contained the first botanical descriptions of many species. Seventy years after his death, *Science* described Elliott as the "Father of Southern Botany." In 1901, Frank Lamson-Scribner wrote the following about Elliott's *Sketch*: "Not until one has prepared a book where almost every line contains a statement of fact learned from original observation can one fully appreciate the amount of patience and labor involved in the preparation of such a work as the *Sketch of the Botany of South Carolina and Georgia* . . . today it remains indispensable to the working systemic botanists of our country."[9]

---

[9] *Joseph Ewan, "Editors Introduction", In: 1971 reprint of A Sketch of the Botany of South Carolina and Georgia in Classica Botanica Americana (series) Hafner Publishing Company: New York. 1971. page v.*

Lyons Road

Chelone lyonii*
John Lyons
1765–1814

John Lyons, also known as John Lyon and John Lion, was born in Forfarshire, Scotland, but very little is known about his early life, and there are no known images of him. He came to the United States as a gardener or perhaps as an indentured gardener for William Hamilton. Hamilton owned a 300 acre estate just outside of Philadelphia, near the Schuylkill River, known today as Fairmont Park. In 1796, Lyons was overseeing the gardens on the Hamilton estate. To furnish the estate gardens with different types of plantings, he discovered new species by traveling into the Allegheny Mountains of Western Pennsylvania, as far south as Florida, and as far west as Nashville. Most of his travels were to the southern Appalachians and western North Carolina.

Lyons was known as a "plant hunter" and an exporter of plants to Europe. During his time in the United States, he kept a journal recounting his travels and discoveries. The journal was edited by Joseph and Nesta Ewan and published in 1963 as *John Lyon, Nurseryman and Plant Hunter, and His Journal, 1799-1814* by the American Philosophical Society. The contents reveal that Lyons collected plants from several North Carolina

---

*Courtesy Alan Cressler, Lady Bird Johnson Wildflower Center

mountain areas, including Roan, Grandfather, and Pilot Mountains. The Linville River and North Cove were also favorite collecting places. In 1807, Lyons found Michaux's *Rhododendron catawbiense* on a high precipice near the headwaters of the Catawba River, east of Asheville, North Carolina.

"Lyons is credited with introducing more than thirty new plants into horticulture. One of the plants, fetterbush (*Pieris floribunda*), discovered at Pilot Mountain, September 16, 1807, is planted as far north as Boston because of its hearty nature and is prized for its beautiful floral displays. Other American plants Lyons introduced to Europe include the *Magnolia, Halesia, Gordonia, Stewartia,* and *Pinckneya*. Lyons established several garden sites in Philadelphia where he kept and cared for the plants scheduled for shipment to Europe. Some of his shipments were orders from wealthy patrons; other plants were sold at auction. In 1806, he published a catalog of available plants prior to one of his auctions. The catalog included a large quantity of one-year-old seedlings in pots and ten lots of 50 different types of seeds."[10]

Lyons is considered by some to be one of the most overlooked botanists of his time. His plant collecting trips followed in the footsteps of such well-known botanists as William Bartram, André and Francois Michaux, Asa Gray, and Moses Ashley Curtis. "He was among the intrepid plant collectors who first penetrated the southern mountains during the late 18th and early 19th centuries to catalogue the diverse and not infrequently endemic flora that flourishes here."[11] Frederick Pursh, a leading American botanist, named *Chelone lyonii*, pink turtlehead, in John Lyon's honor. John Loudon, a Scottish chronicler of arboriculture and agriculture, reported that Lyons' plant

---

[10] George Ellison, "John Lyon (1765–1814): Scottish Explorer, Plant Collector & Nurseryman, *Chinquapin: The Newsletter of the Southern Appalachian Botanical Society,* 14, no. 1 (Spring 2006): 29.
[11] Ibid.

shipments to Europe were "by far the greatest collection of American trees and shrubs ever brought to England at one time by one individual."[12]

For Lyons, as well as for other botanists of his time, collecting plant specimens was challenging and dangerous. When his horse would get loose, Lyons would be forced to travel by foot, and he would usually get lost due to poor trails and no maps. This often resulted in endless wandering and going without food or the comfort of a bed. On another adventure, he was bitten by a dog in the back woods, and his only option was to use natural remedies to prevent the wound from getting infected.

Silas McDowell, historian and agriculturist from Macon County, North Carolina, wrote in the early autumn of 1814, that Lyons contracted a "bilious fever" during his "strenuous travels." McDowell, who described Lyons as a "small man of fine countenance," explained that Lyons, who was very ill, traveled from Black Mountain to Asheville, where he took a room in the Eagle Hotel. A blacksmith named Johnston, who had befriended Lyons during an earlier visit to Asheville, took care of him. On the day of his death, Lyons noticed "a beautiful sunset—the last I shall ever behold" and asked Johnston to take him to the window, so he could look out. After the sun sank out of sight, Lyons said, "Beautiful world, farewell. Friend Johnston lay me down upon my bed," which Johnston did, whereupon Lyons fell asleep and died.[13]

Lyons was buried in Asheville and his tombstone, barely legible today, is one of the earliest engraved stones in the area. After his death, his remains were moved twice, from the Old Burial ground to the Old Presbyterian Graveyard to a final resting place in the Riverside Cemetery in Asheville. The remains of Thomas Wolfe and other prominent Asheville residents are also buried in this cemetery.

---

[12] *Ibid.*
[13] *Ibid. 30.*

Michaux Road

Francois André Michaux*
1770–1855

In 1746, André Michaux was born in Satory, south of Versailles, France. He married in 1769, but his wife died within a year of their marriage while giving birth to their son, François André Michaux. Michaux took up the study of botany after his wife's death and eventually became a student of Bernard de Jussieu, the foremost French botanist of the time. In 1782, he was sent by the French government on a botanical mission to Persia. During this trip, he used his knowledge of herbs to cure the Shah of a dangerous illness. After three years and a number of perilous events, he returned to France with seeds and plant specimens. Louis XVI appointed Michaux to the post of Royal Botanist. In 1785, he traveled to the United States on France's first investigation of North American plants with possible medicinal or agricultural value. In 1786, Michaux established a botanical garden of 111 acres near what is now North Charleston, South Carolina. From here he made expeditions to various parts of North America, discovering and naming many North American species. Between 1785 and 1791, he shipped ninety

---

Photo courtesy of the Hunt Institute for Botanical Documentation, Carnegie Mellon University, Pittsburgh, Pa.

cases of plants and many seeds to France. At the same time, he introduced many species from other parts of the world to America, including the *Camellia sasanqua*, tea olive, crepe myrtle, and ginkgo. After the French monarchy collapsed, Michaux, the "Royal Botanist," lost his source of income, so he lobbied the American Philosophical Society to support his explorations. Although he was shipwrecked on his return trip to France in 1796, most of the specimens he was transporting managed to survive, as did he. He is believed to have died in Madagascar in 1802.

Michaux's legacy lives on in the names of many plants that grow in North Carolina, including the Carolina Lily (*Lilium michauxii*) and Michaux's saxifrage (*Saxifraga michauxii*). In 2003, the North Carolina Legislature made the Carolina Lily the official state wildflower. In reviewing *Gray's Manual of Botany, 7th edition*, Rodney True noted that André Michaux was responsible for naming 24 new genera and 293 new species of flowering plants found in the publication.[14] In his lifetime, Michaux collected and studied plants from Florida to Hudson Bay and west to Missouri.

François accompanied his father to the United States when he was a teenager and became an accomplished botanist in his own right. François's three-volume *Histoire des arbres forestiers de l'Amérique septentrionale* contains the results of his explorations and provides the scientific classification of the principal American timber trees north of Mexico and east of the Rocky Mountains.

François published his monumental work, *The North American Sylva*, first in French and then in English, between 1811 and 1819. With illustrations by Pierre-Joseph Redouté and Pancrace Bessa, two masters of botanical art, his work soon became a landmark in American botanical literature and the foundation for the study of American forests.

---

[14] *Daniel Stowe Botanical Garden (2013). Michaux Discoveries. Retrieved from http://www.michaux.org/photos.htm (accessed 5 May 2016).*

A letter found in Totten's correspondence files addressed to the Barton Family, who had recently purchased a home at 1500 Michaux Road, celebrates the botanists. The Barton's young son apparently complained about the difficulty of pronouncing the name of the street, so Totten wrote back saying: "I am also enclosing a short reprint that gives a brief outline of the work of André Michaux and his son, François André Michaux, in hope that it may help your fine son to appreciate a bit of the work of two very worthy French botanists of a long time ago. The area around Chapel Hill is so rich in plant and animal life and so many red-blooded boys of the past have roamed these hills and have added to their interest, physique, and enjoyment of life itself. . . . Yes I hope and believe in time your son will not only tolerate the name of Michaux Road, but will also be proud of it."

Velma Road

Velma Dare Matthews*
1904–1958

Velma Road is named for Dr. Coker's doctoral student, Velma Dare Matthews. Matthews was born in 1904 in Burlington, North Carolina, and raised in High Point, North Carolina. She received her undergraduate degree from the North Carolina College for Women (now University of North Carolina at

---

*Photo courtesy of Coker College.

Greensboro) and her M.A. in 1927 and Ph.D. in 1930 from the University of North Carolina at Chapel Hill. Of Coker, Matthews once said, "Dr. Coker had the rare ability to inspire students, to find out more about themselves and to believe in the importance of what they were doing." Coker was a major influence on her accomplishments, which were impressive. [15]

She became a professor of biology at Coker College and for twenty-two years served as the chair of the Coker College Biology Department. A prominent scientist, she authored numerous scientific publications and held leadership positions in a number of scientific organizations. From 1946 to 1947, Matthews served as the first woman president of the South Carolina Academy of Science. The University of North Carolina Herbarium has catalogued approximately 400 vascular plant specimens collected by Matthews, and it is quite possible that more of her specimens will be found in the Herbarium archives. Like Coker and Totten, Matthews was primarily a mycologist.

In the 1958 Coker College Yearbook, she was described as being "beautifully feminine . . . in her blue hat that matched her blue eyes . . . Dr. Matthews was lovely, not only in appearance but also in life. She valued her relationships with people and loved growing things, especially camellias." At her memorial in 1958, mourners paid tribute to her charm, vivaciousness and intelligence. She inspired students and was dedicated not only to the college but to the community of Hartsville, South Carolina.

---

[15] *University of North Carolina Herbarium, William Chambers Coker. Paper Published after Coker's death (June 27, 1953).*

Wood Circle

Carroll E. Wood, Jr.*
1921–2009

Carroll Emory Wood grew up in Salem, Virginia, where his father was a pharmacist and his mother a teacher. His early interest in natural history, encouraged by his parents, evolved after high school into an inclination towards botany but with a sustained interest in butterflies. He graduated from Roanoke College and then completed his master's degree at the University of Pennsylvania. During graduate school, he was already collecting extensively, working on local flora with a special emphasis on carnivorous plants. Military service during World War II interrupted his academic career, but even during this period he continued his interest in collecting plants, sometimes while in uniform and sometimes while on leave.

After military service, Wood returned to graduate school, completing a Ph.D. at the University of California at Berkeley and, at the same time, studying under Professor Merritt Fernald at Harvard University. His first academic appointment was as an assistant professor at the University of North Carolina at Chapel Hill. He then went on to Harvard to become associate

---

Photo courtesy of the Arnold Arboretum Horticultural Library of Harvard University, © President and Fellows of Harvard College. Arnold Arboretum Archives.

curator of the Arnold Arboretum and, later, a professor. Dr. Wood brought a mind of great precision to the field of plant systematics, focusing on the diverse flora of the southeastern United States. As a faculty member at Harvard, he appreciated the opportunity to work in the largest private herbarium in the world with several outstanding botanical libraries, the extensive living collections of the Arnold Arboretum, and many specialized collections in paleobotany, economic botany, and plant anatomy. Wood developed a broad biological approach to plant description that emphasized the genus rather than the species as the unit of study. The result of his work was a floristic synthesis of the diverse flora of the Southeastern United States, from the Carolinas to Florida and westward to Arkansas and Louisiana. His research for a *Generic Flora of the Southeastern United States*, took a biological approach to the description of plants, including their evolutionary history, ecology, geographic distribution, and economic uses. Although Wood wrote many of the early descriptions, he soon recruited a host of collaborators, including graduate and postdoctoral students, his herbarium colleagues at Harvard, and other professional colleagues outside of the institution. A selection of drawings from the *Generic Flora of the Southeastern United States*, based on Wood's dissections of fresh or fluid preserved material, was published as a *Student's Atlas of Flowering Plants*. Perhaps his most visible legacy was *Plant Systematics: A Phylogenetic Approach*, a textbook of plant classification produced by a cohort of his students whom he had shepherded into the modern era of molecular and phylogenetic systematics.

    His students remember Wood for his encyclopedic mind and seriousness of purpose. He also possessed a wry sense of humor, employing comic anecdotes and plays on words. He was a stickler for grammar and, because of this, was sometimes referred to as the "Supervisor of Punctuation." Although he was dedicated to botanical order and semantic precision, his office was usually in a state of clutter and referred to by his students as "Wood's Hole."

As a teacher, Wood was known for accommodating individual student needs through personalized tutorials, his willingness to make material available at all hours, and his enthusiasm for field study. Wood was affiliated with several scientific societies, notably the New England Botanical Society.

In retirement, Wood continued his editorial work and remained interested in horticulture, an enthusiasm originally nurtured by his mother. Wood, like Coker, was a valued source of information about gardens and gardening for friends and neighbors in Boston's South End. When Carroll Wood died of a heart attack, at the age of eighty-eight, people remembered him with great affection.[15]

Final Development Phase of Coker Hills

Dr. Totten accepted the challenge from Coker College to lead one of the finest developments in Chapel Hill. He could not have thought of doing anything more meaningful, even at age sixty-eight. He knew this opportunity would be one that would allow him to make an important contribution to the educational institution founded by the Coker family, and one held in such high esteem by Coker himself. He also believed the neighborhood would be a lasting legacy to his dear friend and colleague.

Totten's role in directing the development of the neighborhood was often a challenging one, fraught with delays caused, in part, by unfortunate geology and bad weather. Still, he worked

---

[15] *Information for this profile of Carroll Wood was obtained from an obituary published on the Harvard Gazette's website on February 17, 2011. It states that the obituary was read and recorded at a Meeting of the Faculty of Arts and Sciences on February 1, 2011, and was prepared by Robert E. Cook, Norton G. Miller, Donald H. Pfizer, and P. Barry Tomlinson, Chair.*

tirelessly, day and night, to ensure the timely completion of Coker Hills. By the early 1970's most of the lots were sold, homes were built, and neighbors were bonding. With Totten's energy on the wane and his wife continuing to experience more health issues, Totten retired from the Chapel Hill Board of Realtors in 1971. Among Totten's many accomplishments, he felt privileged to see the completion of Coker Hills. On January 22, 1974, Addie Totten passed away, and on February 9, 1974, Totten passed away at age 82. Coker Hills will forever remain a part of Totten's legacy.

One of the first homes being built in Coker Hills
Photo courtesy of the Masson Family

4//Coker Hills Architects, Builders, and Homes

He who loves an old house never loves in vain. — Isabel La Howe Conant

Most of the homes in Coker Hills were built from the early 1960's into the early 1970's and reflect both traditional and mid-century modernist architecture. The neighborhood was planned and completed as a relatively affluent neighborhood, nestled within a natural environment. Many of the homes were designed by award-winning architects, some of whom were graduates from the North Carolina State University School of Design, today known as the College of Design. These architects were greatly influenced by their faculty, mentors, and other well-known architects such as Frank Lloyd Wright.

    As Coker Hills developed, owners, architects, project supervisors, and builders worked together to complete the homes making Coker Hills what it is today. Most of the custom home builders were regional builders, building a few homes each year. From year-to-year, builders tried to retain their teams of craftsmen, as this provided more consistent and higher quality workmanship with each new home. Builders purchased many of their materials locally at businesses like Huggins Hardware which was located on West Franklin Street, Fitch Lumber and Hardware in Carrboro, West Durham Lumber Company, and the Triangle Brick Company, a leading brick manufacturer established in 1956 with headquarters in Durham, North Carolina. Slate used in many Coker Hills' homes came from the Buckingham Slate Company in Arvonia, Virginia. The company was founded in 1867 in the James River Basin region, and Buckingham slate was prized for its beauty and durability. Thomas Jefferson was one of the first Americans to recognize the value and architectural beauty of Buckingham slate.

This chapter highlights many of the architects and builders of homes in Coker Hills and also many of the modernist and traditional homes in the neighborhood. Although information on every home in Coker Hills was not available, every home in Coker Hills holds a special place in the history of the neighborhood. Every original owner in Coker Hills is listed in Appendix 3, along with the Coker Hills Lot Map (Appendix 4). The information is as accurate as humanly possible.

The Architects

Great architecture has only two enemies: water and stupid men.
— Richard Nickel

Architecture is one of the "necessary" arts, always with the capacity to reach the peak of creative impulses but also tempered by the need to function. Architecture physically defines an area, making it different from any other and affecting the way people regard their environment.
— Tony Wrenn and Elizabeth Mulloy, America's Forgotten Architecture

James Lorn "J.L." Beam, Jr.
1918-2010

J. L. was born in Gaston County, North Carolina and became a well-known architect in Cherryville and Gastonia, North Carolina. He attended Lenoir-Rhyne College and graduated from the North Carolina State University School of Design. He also attended the Naval Design School at the Massachusetts Institute of Technology. During his career he designed many businesses, churches, residences, and schools in North Carolina. Beam designed the Summer House at 300 North Elliott Road.

Arthur Ralph Cogswell, FAIA
1930-2010

Arthur Cogswell was born in Jacksonville, Florida and graduated from the University of North Carolina at Chapel Hill in 1952 with a degree in drama. He served in the U.S. Air Force during the Korean War, and after that conflict he attended North Carolina State University School of Design, graduating in 1959 with a degree in Architecture. He initially worked for Don Stewart at City Planning and Architecture Associates (CPAA) in Chapel Hill before opening his own firm in 1962. In 1964, he hired Werner Hausler. The two had been college friends, and in 1967 they became partners in Cogswell/Hausler, an architectural firm that flourished for several decades. One of Cogswell's professors at North Carolina State University was George Matsumoto, who greatly influenced Cogswell's studies and future work. Matsumoto was one of the many distinguished professors who came to the North Carolina State University School of Design. As well as teaching future architects, he also designed many homes in the Triangle area. "Matsumoto had the most profound and lasting effect on North Carolina architecture. Matsumoto described himself as a minimal or small house architect who hated wasted labor; although this concept did not stop him from participating in many large exterior and interior design projects."[1] Like Matsumoto, Cogswell left a legacy of modernist homes and buildings. The advent of his career coincided perfectly with the early development in Coker Hills, and he designed many homes in the neighborhood, including his own home at 308 North Elliott Road. Some of the homes identified as Cogswell and/or Cogswell/Hausler designs in the neighborhood include the Hill House at 205 Wood Circle, the Koch House at 401 Clayton Road, the Philas House at 1704 Curtis Road, the Pickett House at 404 Clayton Road, the Prothro House at 305 North Elliott, the Rice House at 311 Clayton Road, the Royal House at 1703 Allard Road, and the Townend House at 411 Clayton Road.

Cogswell also designed the Ridgefield Townhomes, a Chapel Hill affordable housing project. In 1971, Cogswell/Hausler received the Award of Merit for this design from the North Carolina Chapter of the American Institute of Architects (AIA). In making this award, the jury recognized the difficulty of designing an affordable housing project within the typical fiscal constraints. They admired the simplicity and treatment of the design, the careful siting of the townhomes, and the landscaping, all of which evoked a sense of pride for its residents. The same year Cogswell/Hausler won another Award of Merit from the same Chapter for Fire Station Three located on the corner of North Elliott Road and East Franklin Street in Chapel Hill. The jury commented on the successful handling of the project, the unpretentious design, and the careful attention to the building site to minimize the possible obtrusive effect of the structure in a residential neighborhood. The jury also commented on the crisp and careful detail of the design.

In 1972, Cogswell was named a Fellow of the AIA; at the time he was the youngest architect to have received this honor.

---

[1] *George Matsumoto Papers 1945-1991, MC 00042, Special Collections Department, D.H. Hill Library, North Carolina State University, Raleigh, NC.*

He was nominated for the AIA North Carolina Kamphoefner Award in 2010. In 2012, Cogswell received posthumously, the Kamphoefner Award (named for the first Dean of the School of Design at North Carolina State University). His career exemplified Kamphoefner's conviction that an architect's social responsibilities were as important in a project as was the design. Cogswell was known as the consummate professional with a strong sense of humility and humanity. In his later years, he focused his efforts on developing an innovative process to relieve famine in Libya.

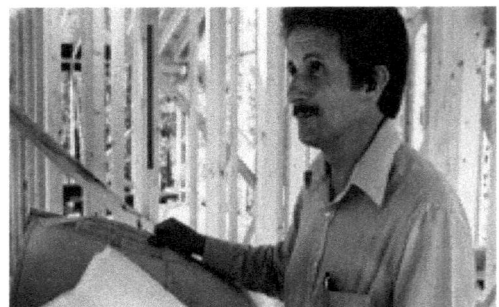

Jon Andre Condoret
1934-2010

Jon Andre Condoret was born in Algiers, Algeria. He graduated from L'École Spéciale d'Architecture in Paris with a Bachelor of Arts Degree in Architecture in 1959. Three years later, he came to North Carolina to work with architect Archie Royal Davis. Davis was known for his designs of the Carolina Inn and the Morehead Planetarium on the University of North Carolina campus. In 1967, Condoret formed Winn/Condoret with partner Sumner Winn, and then joined Don Stewart at City Planning and Architecture Associates (CPAA). Condoret eventually formed his own practice, designing strikingly modern homes in Chapel Hill, Durham, and other areas. In 1992, Condoret designed the Caring House for adult patients receiving cancer treatment at the Duke Comprehensive Cancer Center. In 1985, Condoret provided the architectural design for the remodel of the Winslow House at 403 Clayton Road.

Gary Giles, AIA
1939-

Gary Giles graduated in 1966 from North Carolina State University with a degree in Architecture from the School of Design. After graduation, he joined the architectural firm of Ballard, McKim & Sawyer in Wilmington, North Carolina. While there, he worked on various residential and commercial projects. In 1972, Giles partnered with Joe Nassif in Chapel Hill, North Carolina and their firm became Giles/Nassif Associates. In 1984, Giles began a solo practice, Gary Giles, Architect, AIA. Since 1987, he has partnered with Josh Gurlitz at the award-winning GGA Architects. Some of their contributions to Chapel Hill include the Franklin Hotel and the Chapel Hill Aquatic Center at Homestead Park. Giles designed the Rugen House at 1502 Velma Road.

Joe Hakan
1926-2006

Joe Hakan, a native of Joplin, Missouri, graduated in 1949 from the Duke University Engineering School, but he was a long-standing University of North Carolina fan, and he left his mark on many local landmarks. He began his career at the University of North Carolina at Chapel Hill and became the University's Chief Engineer for campus construction. His campus projects included the tower and facilities for WUNC-TV and the sundial in front of the Morehead Planetarium. In 1963, Hakan started his own architectural firm, Hakan/Corley & Associates. He cared about aesthetics and traveled to Italy for inspiration and finishes when designing the Siena Hotel in Chapel Hill. In 1982, his firm designed the Dean E. Smith Center, home of the Carolina men's basketball team. During the construction, Joe gave each worker a Carolina blue hard hat to show his/their loyalty to the university. In Raleigh, he played a part in designing the Crabtree Valley Mall. Former Raleigh Mayor Smedes York said, "Joe had an idea a minute." Paul Hardin, University of North Carolina at Chapel Hill Chancellor (1988-1995), said Joe was like Mr. Chapel Hill and Mr. UNC, he was very loyal to both town and gown. He designed his own home in Coker Hills at 1910 Allard Road and the Clements House at 1603 Curtis Road.

Harwell Hamilton Harris, FAIA
1903-1990

Harwell Hamilton Harris, FAIA, was born in Redlands, California and grew up in the Imperial Valley area, graduating from San Bernardino High School. He attended Pomona College but left after a year to study sculpture at the Otis Art Institute in Los Angeles, now the Otis College of Art and Design. He studied drawing and painting with Stanton MacDonald-Wright at the Art Student League. However, after he visited the Frank Lloyd Wright Hollyhock House in Los Angeles, his career goals changed from sculpture to architecture. Harris pursued his architectural studies at the University of California at Berkeley but never graduated. Instead, he found employment with Richard Neutra and Rudolf Schindler, both considered pioneers of modernist architecture. Neutra discouraged Harris from attending formal classes in architecture and to learn by doing. In 1933, Harris established his own independent practice in Los Angeles. His first commissions were for smaller homes, and he applied modernist principles learned from Neutra and Schindler. In 1937, Harris was commissioned to design a home for John Entenza, the editor of *California Arts and Architecture*. Harris' designs were known for their sensitivity to a site, clean fluid spaces, and a thoughtful use of materials, all characteristics of the American Arts and Crafts movement. In his residential designs, he created a tension and continuum between exterior and interior with continuous roof lines, and the design of the interior space based on the cruciform plan. In 1943, Harris joined the School of Architecture at Columbia. In 1952, he became the Dean at the School of Architecture at the University of Texas. Although he lacked an architectural degree and administrative experience, he was quite successful at expanding the school's program and improving the student educational experience. In 1962, he moved to Raleigh, North Carolina, where he established a private architectural practice and joined the faculty at the School of Design at North Carolina State University. He retired as a faculty member in 1973 but continued to practice from his home studio in Raleigh until his death in 1990. Harris designed the Lindahl House at 305 Clayton Road.

Werner Hausler, AIA
1933-1999

Werner Hausler graduated from Cornell University in 1954 and served in the US Air Force. In 1956, Werner became an early practitioner of using the computer in architectural design. His work in this area was supported by a grant from the U.S.

Department of Housing and Urban Development. In 1962, he graduated from the North Carolina State University School of Design where he received a Gold Medal for Excellence as the Editor of the *School of Design Journal*. From 1962-64, he worked in the University of North Carolina at Chapel Hill Planning Division. Werner first met Arthur Cogswell when they were students at North Carolina State University. In 1964, Werner joined Arthur Cogswell's architectural firm, and three years later they formed the partnership of Cogswell/Hausler. Werner's architectural designs are found in many buildings in Chapel Hill and in North Carolina. In Coker Hills, some of Werner and Arthur Cogswell's designs include the Philas House at 1704 Curtis Road and the Townend House at 411 Clayton Road. A number of his residential designs received AIA as well as other design awards. From 1990-1994, Werner and his wife, Lyn McClay, worked together at DesignSpec Inc. in Chapel Hill.

Elizabeth Bobbitt Lee, FAIA
1928-2010

Elizabeth "Lib" Bobbitt Lee was a pioneer in North Carolina architecture. Born in Lumberton, North Carolina, Lib was exceptionally good in math and graduated from Salem College in Winston-Salem, North Carolina. In 1952, she became the first woman to graduate from the newly-established North Carolina State University School of Design. She was the second woman to be licensed by the North Carolina Board of Architecture and one of the first women to actively practice architecture in North Carolina.

After graduation, she worked for William Coleman in Kinston, North Carolina. She moved to New York to work for Skidmore, Owings and Merrill, but in the late 1950's, she moved back to Lumberton and partnered with Ronald Thompson to form Lee Thompson Architects. When Thompson retired, the firm became Elizabeth B. Lee, Architect. For several decades, Lib was active in the North Carolina Chapter of the AIA, and she held nearly every position in the chapter hierarchy, including serving as President in 1979 and as the South Atlantic Region Director of the AIA. Lib designed many notable homes and commercial projects including the Robeson County Courthouse in Lumberton and a number of schools in the state. Lib endowed a scholarship for an outstanding architectural student at North Carolina State University. In Coker Hills, Lib designed the Sears House at 1728 Allard Road.

Joseph Lee "Joe" Nassif
1933-

Joe Nassif was raised in Laurinburg, North Carolina and in 1955 graduated from Notre Dame with a degree in Civil Engineering. He returned to North Carolina to attend North Carolina State University, and in 1966 he graduated with a degree in Architecture from the School of Design and joined Cogswell/Hausler. In 1972, he partnered with Gary Giles, and their firm became Giles/Nassif Associates. He later formed a solo architectural practice. From 1979-1985, Nassif served as the Mayor of Chapel Hill. In 2000, he retired from his practice but continues to work on consulting projects. While at Cogswell/Hausler, Nassif was the Project Manager for several Coker Hills homes, including the Koch House at 401 Clayton Road, Philas House at 1704 Curtis Road and the Townend House at 411 Clayton Road.

Thomas Michael Dillon O'Shea
1925-2013

Thomas Michael Dillon O'Shea was born in Trenton, New Jersey, and his family moved to North Carolina when he was nine months old. He attended the Durham public schools and graduated from the University of North Carolina at Chapel Hill. He served during World War II as a navigator in the U.S. Air Force. In 1949, he married Charlotte Tucker and worked for the Tucker Motor Co. and then Durham Realty & Insurance, which later became Southland Associates. In 1967, the family moved to Raleigh, and he attended and graduated from the North Carolina State University School of Design. He practiced residential architecture in North Carolina until his retirement. O'Shea designed the Lester and Betty Ball House at 1707 Audubon Road.

Warren Tobin Savage, III, AIA
1939-

In 1964, Warren Tobin (Toby) Savage graduated with a degree in architecture from Auburn University. Three of his professors at Auburn had North Carolina State University School of Design connections. They were helpful when he moved to Chapel Hill, as Savage was offered a position with Cogswell/Hausler. While at Cogswell/Hausler, he worked with the architectural team on many projects including Fire Station Three at the corner of North Elliott Road and East Franklin Street. The fire station won a Merit Design Award from the North Carolina AIA in 1971. In 1973, he joined Haskins Rice Architects in Raleigh, North Carolina, and became a principal. The firm's name was changed to Haskins Rice Savage and Pearce. Savage formed Rairden Savage Architects before joining O'Brien/Atkins in 1999. Savage was the project architect for O'Brien/Atkins on the $500 million Raleigh-Durham International Airport Terminal C Replacement and Expansion. In 2013, Savage began to consult part-time, focusing on the modernization of existing buildings.

Brian Shawcroft, AIA
1929-

Brian Shawcroft was raised in Nottingham, England. He graduated from the West Essex Technical College and School of Art in 1953 with an ARIBA degree. He worked in the city planning and historic records sections of the Nottingham government. He interned for Tomei and Maxwell in London and latter Slater Uren and Pike, and Page & Steele in Toronto. In 1960, he worked with Eduardo Catalano in Cambridge, Massachusetts, while completing a joint Masters in Architecture degree at MIT and Harvard University. One of his projects while working with Catalano was the Julliard School of Music in New York City. In 1960, Henry Kamphoefner recruited Shawcroft to be an Associate Professor of Architecture in the School of Design at North Carolina State University. While teaching architectural design and photography, Shawcroft also designed many classic modernist homes in the Triangle area. Shawcroft designed commercial buildings while working with Holloway-Reeves and as a principal at Shawcroft-Taylor. Shawcroft's career as an architect spans more than six decades. In 1991, he was awarded North Carolina State University's Kamphoefner Prize for his integrity and devotion to the modern movement in architecture. His photographs and architectural renderings have been exhibited many times. The Brian Shawcroft Papers are now housed in the

North Carolina State University Special Collections. Shawcroft designed the Judith Watkins House at 1708 Curtis Road.

William Van Easton Sprinkle
1906-1965

William Van Easton Sprinkle was a native of Mocksville, North Carolina. He earned his undergraduate degree at Duke University in 1927 and completed studies in architecture at Yale in 1928. For two years he worked in a New York architectural firm for free, while painting watercolors to earn his keep. In 1930, he returned to Durham, North Carolina, and worked with architect Howard Haines gaining experience in residential design. In 1934, Sprinkle opened his own studio and completed a number of commissions for Duke University. Sprinkle designed many fine residences in the Chapel Hill and Durham areas. In Coker Hills, Sprinkle designed the Wysor House at 304 North Elliott Road.

Anne Bickett Parker Stevens, AIA
1921-2007

Anne Stevens was born in Marshville, North Carolina and grew up in Albemarle, North Carolina. Her dream was to study architecture, but her interest was not encouraged by her mother. Setting her architectural pursuits aside, she studied mathematics and art at the Woman's College of the University of North Carolina (now University of North Carolina at Greensboro). Desiring to continue her education, Anne applied to Columbia University in New York, but she was denied admission, most likely because she was female. She was admitted to Syracuse University, and when Columbia began to admit female students to their architectural program, she enrolled and graduated with a Bachelor's Degree in Architecture. In 1941, while at Syracuse, the Central New York Chapter of the American Institute of Architects presented her with an award for Excellence in Design. She worked for the U.S. Army during WWII on the design of Camp Davis in Holly Ridge, North Carolina. Anne's family was prominent in the state; her uncle was North Carolina Governor Luther Hodges. In 1945, she married Jack Stevens and moved to Jack's home state of Pennsylvania settling in Pittsburgh. While in Pittsburgh, Anne worked with an architectural firm, and in the mid-1950's, Jack and Anne started the Jack Stevens

Building Company, a design/build firm, with Anne, the designer and Jack, the contractor. In 1968, they moved to Burlington, North Carolina and then to Chapel Hill. In 1974, they returned to Charlotte and moved to Pinehurst in 1979 where they continued to design and build homes. Jack died in 1981, and in 1983 Anne moved to Surf City, North Carolina where she designed homes and enjoyed her love of painting. According to former client Mary Whittier, Anne and her husband built over 600 homes during their careers. Because of her affinity for developing lists to guide her through her various construction projects, Anne loved to get yellow-lined note pads as Christmas gifts. This became a long-standing family joke. Anne was known to watch every detail of the project, no matter how seemingly insignificant, and she would not hesitate to show the workers how something should be done or request the work be redone. Anne demanded the highest standard of quality and took great pride in becoming a licensed builder after her husband passed away. She often said she was the first licensed female builder in North Carolina. Anne and Jack Stevens built several homes in Coker Hills, including the Crounse House at 1730 Allard Road, the Monroe House at 404 Lyons Road and the Whittier House at 402 Lyons Road.

J. Knox Tate, IV, AIA
1944-

Knox Tate was born in Lexington, Virginia. He received a B.S. in Civil Engineering from Duke University in 1966. After four years in the U.S. Navy, he went on to earn his B.A. in Architecture from the University of Tennessee, School of Design. Early in his career, Tate worked with Arthur Cogswell and JP Goforth. He also taught structure and design courses at the North Carolina State University School of Design. He served as a Chapel Hill Historic District Commissioner for ten years and as Chair of the Historic District Commission for four years. He practices in Chapel Hill as J. Knox Tate, IV, Architect. He is married to Stella Waugh, whose father was architect Terry Waugh. In 1968, Tate worked with builder JP Goforth on the design of the Sidney Louis Eastman House at 1710 Michaux Road.

Arthur Norman Tuttle, Jr. AIA
1931-2004

Arthur Tuttle went to high school in Richmond, Virginia and Tilton, New Hampshire. He graduated from Virginia Polytechnic Institute with a Bachelor of Science degree in 1952. He served in the Korean War as a draftsman with the U.S. Army Corps of Engineers. In 1956, he received an M.A. in Architecture from Princeton University. He also attended the University of North Carolina at Chapel Hill School of City and Regional Planning. Tuttle worked for Marcellus Wright in Richmond, Virginia; McLaughlin and Jandl in Princeton, New Jersey; Ivan Altman in Richmond, Virginia; and Jim Webb and George Cobb in Chapel Hill. He served as the Director of Planning for the University of North Carolina at Chapel Hill from 1959-1969. He then accepted a position at the University of Oklahoma as Director of Architectural Engineering Services and also taught architecture at the university. The AIA named the Arthur N. Tuttle, Jr. Graduate Fellowship in Health Facility Planning and Design in his honor. Tuttle designed the Hindsdale House at 1405 Michaux Road.

James (Jim) Webb
1908-2000

John Webb
1910-1997

The Webb Brothers, Jim and John, were both born in Aguascalientes, Mexico where their father worked for the Guggenheim family's American Mine. In 1937, Jim received a Degree in Architecture from the University of California at Berkeley. After graduating, he served in the U.S. Army and during service was diagnosed with tuberculosis. He recovered from this illness at the Army Hospital in Colorado. Following his discharge, he received a Master's Degree in City Planning from MIT in 1946. After graduation he worked for prominent architect William Wurster in California.

During this time, John Webb also graduated with a Degree in Architecture from the University of California at Berkeley, where William Wurster was one of his professors. "Wurster created the 'Bay Area Style' of architecture, adapting design to the hilly terrain of the San Francisco area, featuring porches, balconies, and patios which extended the living area into the natural environment. Wurster's style has been described as 'livable charm' and 'living beautifully', not just differently."[2] His work influenced the Webbs' future designs.

In 1947, Jim joined the new Department of City and Re-

---

[2] David Weinstein, *Signature Architects of the San Francisco Bay Area*, Gibs Smith Publisher, 2006, page 9.

gional Planning at the University of North Carolina at Chapel Hill, and he remained on the faculty for thirty years. In the late 1950s, Jim founded City Planning and Architecture Associates (CPAA), a local architectural and design firm and recruited architect, Don Stewart, as his partner. While Jim was in Chapel Hill, John was in Detroit working with architect Albert Kahn. In 1964, John moved to Chapel Hill to work with CPAA and several years later, returned to Berkeley. John was known for his work in designing the John F. Kennedy gravesite in Arlington National Cemetery. Jim Webb designed many "Bay area houses" for University of North Carolina faculty, including one for President William Friday. Jim also completed designs for clients in the Research Triangle Park and Appalachian State University. Jim Webb left CPAA in the mid-1970s to begin a solo practice, where he continued until his passing in 2000. Jim Webb designed the Ethel Redney Akin House at 414 Lyons Road.

Louis Sumner Winn, Jr.
1928-2000

Louis Sumner Winn grew up in Worcester, Massachusetts and graduated from Bowdoin College in 1950. After graduation, he joined the U.S. Air Force and served during the Korean War. Following his military service, he studied for a year at the Sorbonne in Paris. He attended the Rhode Island School of Design and graduated with a B.S. in Architecture. In 1960, he moved to Chapel Hill and worked for architect Archie Royal Davis who designed the Carolina Inn and the Morehead Planetarium. In 1967, Winn established a partnership with Jon Condoret, and their firm became Winn/Condoret. Later he joined City Planning and Architecture Associates (CPAA). In 1973, Winn established his solo practice in Chapel Hill. Unfortunately, many of his records and drawings were lost in a house fire in 1994. Winn's residential designs were known for their beautiful corner windows, large brick fireplaces and extended post and beam exterior eaves. Some of the homes Winn designed in Coker Hills include the Barton House at 1500 Michaux Road, the Bell House at 1707 Michaux Road and the Perry House at 311 North Elliott Road.

The Builders*

A house isn't really understandable until it settles into the site: until it's built, furnished and lived in for four or five years. The reality is not on paper but how a building sits on the land, how it relates to trees, to slopes, to water, to gardens.
— Jaquelin T. "Jaque" Robertson, FAIA, FAICP

Robert (Bob) Bacon
1929-

Bob Bacon was born in Massachusetts. From 1947 to 1948 he attended and graduated from the Boston Institute. In 1951, he was drafted and served in the U.S. Army Transportation Corp. In 1955, he joined Techbuilt, a design and manufacturing company of prefabricated, modernist homes. In 1959, Bob formed Deck House with partners, William Berkes, a graduate from the Harvard School of Architecture, and Robert Brownell. Deck House became a national leader in prefab modern homes using post and bean construction, tongue and groove vaulted ceilings and sliding glass doors leading out to a deck. Bacon was the Director of Sales, Berkes the designer, and Brownell served as operations manager. Shortly after they established Deck House, *Better Homes and Gardens* featured the company as providing the best value in modernist home construction. In 1968, Bob moved to North Carolina, and in 1970 formed BoMar Construction with partner, Maurice Pridgen. Around 1980, Bacon became part owner of Hill Country Woodworks. BoMar built the Warren House at 408 Lyons Road

Photos were not available for all builders.

David Lee Curl
1928-2010

David Lee Curl, of Orange Builders, was one of the preeminent area builders of single-family residential homes. He was also a founding member of the Home Builders Association of Durham and Orange Counties. One of the homes he built in Coker Hills is the Sears House at 1728 Allard Road.

Bruce Crumpton
1935-2013

Bruce Wilmot Crumpton grew up in Roxboro, North Carolina. After graduating from Roxboro High School, he earned a B.A. in Business Administration from the University of North Carolina at Chapel Hill in 1957. Bruce became a renowned builder and businessman in Chapel Hill. He was a partner with the firm of Spence, Lester and Crumpton Inc., and later opened his own business, Chapel Hill Communities, Inc. During his involvement with these businesses, Bruce contributed to the construction of several neighborhoods in Chapel Hill including Colony Woods, Briarcliff, Booker Creek, and Timberlyne. Filled with a true passion for his work, Crumpton never truly retired. In fact, he renewed his real estate license only one month prior to his death which occurred after a brief illness at his home in Cape Carteret, North Carolina. One of the custom homes built by Bruce Crumpton in Coker Hills is the Nelson House at 410 Lyons Road.

Carl Ellington
1904-1986

Carl Ellington was born at Pace's Mill on the Haw River in Chatham County, North Carolina. He began his career in commercial construction in the early 1920's and worked on the university's Wilson Library, Manning Hall, and Kenan Stadium. He also worked on the construction of Fort Bragg, North Carolina and the naval station in Elizabeth City, North Carolina before and during World War II. He built many area homes and was in partnership with his brother-in-law, Phillip Sparrow from the late 1940s to the early 1970s. Carl was considered one of the best builders in the area. He built several homes in Coker Hills including the Barton House at 1500 Michaux Road, the Rice House at 311 Clayton Road, and the Via House at 307 Clayton Road.

Lindsey Luther Fogelman
1922-2007

In 1949, E. Judson Pickett and Lindsey Luther Fogelman founded the Delta Construction Company in Durham, North Carolina. In 1957, Pickett founded the Pickett Real Estate Company, and Lindsey Fogelman continued building homes in the Durham and Chapel Hill area. He completed the Wysor House at 304 North Elliott Road and Chapel Hill Fire Station Three.

James Paul (JP) Goforth
1940-1990

James Paul (JP) Goforth grew up on a tenant farm in Statesville, North Carolina. As an undergraduate at the University of North Carolina at Chapel Hill, he worked as a real estate agent to help pay his way through school. By the time he entered the School of Law at the university in 1973, he had formed his own company, Security Building. The homes he built in Coker Hills were constructed during his early years as a custom home builder. Some of these homes include the Bouldin House at 202 North Elliott Road, the Byrd House at 404 North Elliott Road, the Choi House at 1714 Michaux Road, the Conway/Thompson House at 1720 Allard Road, the Eastman House at 1710 Michaux Road, the Falk House at 1711 Allard Road, the Hagadorn House at 405 Lyons Road, the Hubbard House at 1710 Audubon Road, the Locher House at 1713 Audubon Road, and the Scott House at 1711 Audubon Road.

After building custom homes in Coker Hills, Goforth went on to build many homes in other Chapel Hill neighborhoods, such as Coker Hills West, Stoneridge, Ironwoods, Forest Creek, Northwood, and The Oaks II. By the mid-1970s, he was Orange County's largest home builder and his operation quickly spread to Durham County. By the early 1980s, JP owned Triangle Millwork, Chapel Hill Grading, Boyce Supply, and Chapel Hill Electric, all of which supported the building trade. At one time his companies employed more than 180 people. JP seemed to have the Midas touch and weathered the 1980 and 1983 recessions better than his peers. Starting in 1984, JP began to expand his organization in eastern North Carolina, broadening his model of building well-designed, upscale communities. Landfall in Wilmington, North Carolina is an example of one such development. By the early 1990s, however, the US was in yet another economic recession. JP found himself with a substantial investment in land that was no longer viable for development as well as an inventory of unsold homes. His businesses were in debt and taxes were owed on land and houses he could not sell. JP had been a master businessman, but due to health issues, he was no longer able to dedicate every hour of the day to his businesses. His cash flow was now well below what was needed and liquidating assets proved to be difficult. Tragically, at the age of 49, he took his own life.

Goforth was considered one of Chapel Hill's most prominent and influential developers, building many thoughtfully and meticulously designed homes and neighborhoods. He cared about the environment and carefully sited each home on the property, protecting the surrounding vegetation as much as possible. His homes, especially his early custom homes, were exceptionally well built. Mel Rashkis, an original Coker Hills owner said, "Mr. Goforth deserves a lot of credit for all the good he brought to a lot of people and his community."[3]

---

[3] *The Rise and Fall of Chapel Hill's JP Goforth. Chapel Hill Memories, April 15, 2011.*

Herbert Hahn
1932-

Herbert "Bud" Hahn was raised in Birmingham, Alabama where his father was a custom home builder. Bud graduated from Vanderbilt with a degree in chemical engineering. After serving in the U.S. Army, he attended Harvard. Later he received his Ph.D. in finance from the University of North Carolina at Chapel Hill School of Business. While in graduate school, he built several custom traditional style homes in Chapel Hill. His homes included a brick exterior, basement, garage, full-story attic and sometimes included a secret closet. Hahn built the Maher House at 417 Lyons Road.

Don Higgs
1931-

Don Higgs, born in New York City, received his undergraduate and graduate degrees from the University of Maryland. In 1975, he moved to Chapel Hill, became a licensed contractor, and built many homes in the area, including the Coventry townhomes on Weaver Dairy Road in Chapel Hill. He retired in 1993. In Coker Hills, he built the Stehman White Oak House at 419 Clayton Road.

Odis Johnson
1930-

Odis Johnson was born in Orange County, North Carolina and began his building career as a carpenter. By 1954 he had become a custom home builder. He built many homes in Orange, Durham, and Alamance counties, typically building four to five homes a year. Today, his company is known as Odis Johnson Construction and is based in Hillsborough, North Carolina. In Coker Hills, he built the Glenn House at 1705 Michaux Road.

Herman Braxton Lloyd
1914-1991

Herman Braxton Lloyd, born in Orange County, North Carolina, was a local area custom home builder. He attended the University of North Carolina at Chapel Hill and was a member of the football and baseball teams and served in the U.S. Army during WWII. He built over 100 homes in his 40-year career, and several of his homes were in the Coker Hills neighborhood. Herman, his wife, Thelma, and Greensboro architect Ralph Stanford worked together in the design of traditional homes with an emphasis on practicality and efficiency. Lloyd homes featured abundant storage, including built-ins, separation of formal and informal space and low maintenance building materials. Some of his building innovations included the "look through" (a large open area from the kitchen into the family room and a forerunner to the open concept floorplan), the built-in office which could be concealed by sliding panel doors, a hobby space, and the use of low maintenance materials like "brushtex" brick and redwood exteriors. The last ten years of his career were devoted to restoration work and his two favorite restoration projects were the Horace Williams House and the Betty Smith House, both in Chapel Hill's Historic District. He built several homes in Coker Hills including the Breslin House at 1704 Michaux Road and the Summer House at 300 North Elliott Road.

Edward N. Mann Sr.
1909-1992

Edward N. Mann, Sr., known as Eddie, was born in Carrboro, North Carolina. He spent most of his career as a custom home builder and built over a hundred homes in the Chapel Hill area. He specialized in architecturally-designed homes and worked closely with architects like Arthur Cogswell and Louis Sumner Winn. Mann built several homes in Coker Hills including the Pickett House at 404 Clayton, the Prothro House at 306 North

Elliott, the Rashkis House at 415 Clayton and the Tenney House at 315 North Elliott.

Fritz Metz
1944-

Fritz Metz has been a builder since 1972 and a licensed contractor since 1980. He grew up in Pennsylvania and in 1972 moved to Chapel Hill with his wife, who had accepted a position at the University of North Carolina at Chapel Hill. Initially, he worked for a number of local building contractors, including Dennis Howell, Spence, Lester and Crumpton Inc., and JP Goforth. He formed Metz and Dehart Builders, Inc. and then Metz Builders, where he continues to specialize in custom homes, renovations, and remodels. Metz and Dehart built the Rugen House at 1502 Velma Road.

Donald J. Scholz
1920-2000

Donald Scholz had an idea in the late 1940's, when there was a demand for housing by the legions of returning GI's. His idea was to manufacture customized housing at a reasonable cost. Most post war subdivisions had small lots, and the homes were very compact. Scholz decided to change that by using larger lots and larger homes. Scholz, who walked with crutches because of polio, was an engineer by training; a background that played into the design and construction of his homes. He was not a formally-trained architect, but he was influenced by modernist architects like Mies van der Rohe and Frank Lloyd Wright.

Scholz used innovative prefabrication techniques which reduced the cost of homes yet maintained the feel of luxury. The wall panels were constructed in one of seven factories, delivered by truck to the home site and then erected by the company. The designs, which included vaulted ceilings and beams, ample windows and kitchens that were sleek and modern for the era, appealed to many people. In 1969, Scholz was named the Builder of the Year by *Professional Builder* magazine for being a pioneer in modular housing and for being among the first to build and sell prefabricated homes. In 1979, he was inducted into the National Association of Home Builders Hall of Fame. In 2000, Scholz was named one of the 20th century's most influential figures in the residential building industry by *Builder Magazine*. His company was sold but continues to design (not build) homes under the name Scholz Design. The Rashkis House at 415 Clayton Road is a Scholz Design home.

Roy McRee Spratt
1920-2013

Roy Spratt was born in Greenville, South Carolina and graduated from Presbyterian College. He retired in 1964 from the U.S. Air Force as a lieutenant colonel. A year later, he started Spratt Construction and Real Estate. For over twenty-five years he built, sold, and renovated many homes in Chapel Hill. In addition to his interest in building and renovating, he loved to play the saxophone and frequently played with the Fidgety Feet Dixieland Band in Chapel Hill. One of the homes Spratt built in Coker Hills was the Royal House at 1703 Allard Road.

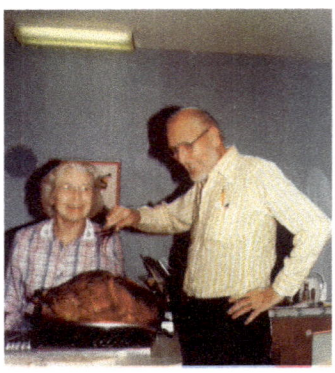

Carlyle John "Lyle" Stehman
1909-1989

Lyle Stehman was raised in Collinsville, Illinois and graduated from the University of Illinois with a degree in chemistry and went on to earn a Ph.D. in Organic Chemistry from Penn State University. For most of his career, he worked for Monsanto, doing research and development work on synthetic fibers. His wife, Ursula, was born in 1909 in Urbana, Illinois. She also attended the University of Illinois and graduated with a degree in music. After graduation, she went to Vienna to perform and to continue to study music. Ursula returned to the United States when she and Lyle married. Throughout her life, she continued to pursue her love of music, whether it was playing the organ, teaching music or performing. Lyle and Ursula designed and built three homes. In 1962, they built their home at 407 Clayton Road. In 1965, Lyle purchased the property at 409 Clayton Road as a birthday present for Ursula, since she loved the white oaks on the property. They designed and built the home at 409 Clayton in 1981. Each of their homes was designed to accommodate their family needs as well as Ursula's instruments, including two pianos and an organ.

C.S. Witt
1924-2007

C.S. Witt of Durham, North Carolina built custom homes and many modernist houses. Witt built the Bell House at 1707 Michaux Road and the Bowles House at 1712 Michaux Road.

Mid-Century Modernist Homes in Coker Hills

The opportunities are unlimited for the design graduates to contribute to the solution of problems in building, design, planning and general construction. — Henry Leveke Kamphoefner

What are these unusual houses in Coker Hills? If it looks a bit different, it's probably a modernist house, a style originating in Germany and made famous by Frank Lloyd Wright, Walter Gropius, Richard Neutra, and others during the 1930's. Modernist designs are characterized by flat or low-pitched roofs, unusual geometry, open floor plans and large windows or other means of bringing in natural light. The modernist movement in residential architecture was cresting into the 1960's, and Coker Hills was no exception. Because of the North Carolina State University School of Design, the Triangle has over 800 modernist houses, many done by North Carolina State University faculty or alumni. North Carolina has the third largest collection of modernist houses in the country, after Los Angeles and New York's Long Island.

Henry Kamphoefner was recruited from the University of Oklahoma by University of North Carolina President Frank Porter Graham in 1948 and was given authority to reorganize what was then called Architectural Engineering at North Carolina State University. Kamphoefner was brilliant and unstoppable, and he brought a new organizational mindset to the school. He increased admission standards and recruited faculty "rock stars" of that era, including George Matsumoto, Terry Waugh, Duncan Stewart, Eduardo Catalano, Jim and Margaret Fitzgibbon, Milton Small and Brian Shawcroft.

He encouraged many of the faculty to practice their art outside of the classroom. Many of the architects who designed houses in Coker Hills were taught by these faculty members. Within a few years, North Carolina State University became a nationally ranked school for modernist architects and architectural training. As a result, in Chapel Hill there are concentrations of modernist homes in the Coker Hills, Lake Forest and Morgan Creek neighborhoods. By 1950, Kamphoefner curated a distinguished guest lecture series at North Carolina State University which brought in nationally known architects like Frank Lloyd Wright, Richard Neutra, Buckminster Fuller and others.

By 1960, modernist design was in full bloom nationwide with buildings such as the sweeping Washington Dulles International Airport, designed by Eero Saarinen, capturing the public's imagination. New modernist houses often had room-to-room intercoms (the internet of that era), custom millwork for "hi-fi," a hide-a-way bar for the popular 5pm martinis and a new innovation, the carport. Demand for the modernist houses shifted in the 1960's in part due to the commercial market. Companies like Deck House manufactured open, solid, post and beam prefab designs featuring tongue-and-groove vaulted ceilings with sliding glass doors. The client would choose the design, and Deck House shipped the parts to the contractor. Locally, C.S. Witt of Durham and BoMar Construction Company built most of these Deck Houses. Other modernist prefab companies included Techbuilt, Lustron and Scholz. These prefabs inspired more than a few Orange County residents to have local architects and/or builders do custom variations on the modernist theme.

Modernist houses are generally considered more works of art than mere shelter and attracted those who appreciated the feeling of living "inside art." In Chapel Hill, a community of many artists, academics and architects, it is no wonder there are so many modernist houses, especially in Coker Hills. Modernist owners truly loved their homes with a passion, and a surprising percentage moved in and never left. Yet, modernism is certainly not for everyone. The failure of modernist design to catch on with homebuyers nationally has always been disappointing to its loyal admirers. The general public tends to buy more traditional designs, except in rare communities like Los Angeles or Palm Springs. Modernist or unconventional houses can be considered somewhat treasonous anomalies to the conservative homeowner mindset. What is "brilliant" to an architecturally-inclined person can often be unsettling to neighbors. Even in liberal Chapel Hill, owners of the first modernist house in town, designed by George Matsumoto, were sued by neighbors all the way to the North Carolina Supreme Court. The owners won and the home remains on Ledge Lane. As one modernist owner said, "People want to be safe, and they want to be like everyone else."

By 1970, the modernist surge was over and the public fell out of love with modernism and moved on to "contemporary," a style borrowing elements from modernism but cutting back on natural light sources, reducing room size and abandoning flat roofs entirely. The College of Design at North Carolina State University remains a top-ranked design school but no longer has the modernist focus. The North Carolina Chapter of the American Institute of Architects maintains the Kamphoefner Prize for career excellence in the modernist tradition, and the newest building at the College of Design is named Kamphoefner Hall. After a thirty year lapse, by the year 2000, modernist houses came back into vogue. Today, approximately fifty modernist houses are built each year in North Carolina.

With thanks to George Smart, Executive Director North Carolina Modernist Houses, www.ncmodernist.org.

Akin House

The Ethel Redney Akin House, 414 Lyons Road, was built in 1967. Ms. Akin moved to Chapel Hill after a career as a nurse supervisor in Chicago. Ms. Akin was 67 at the time the house was planned. The design for the home was the result of architect Jim Webb's vision. In 1976, Ms. Akin sold her home and moved to Southern Pines, North Carolina. Photo by Nicole Alvarez.

Ball House

The Ball House, 1707 Audubon Road, was designed by architect Thomas O'Shea of Raleigh in 1968. Between 1969 and 1970, the builder, possibly JP Goforth, built the home for Dr. and Mrs. Lester and Betty Ball. Dr. Ball was a professor at the University of North Carolina at Chapel Hill, School of Education. Photo by Chase Hanes.

Barton House

The Barton House was built in 1961 for Roger E. and Dorothy Barton at 1500 Michaux Road. Dr. Barton was a faculty member in the School of Dentistry at the University of North Carolina at Chapel Hill. Louis Sumner Winn, Jr. may have been the architect, and the builder was Carl Ellington. Dr. Barton was an organized and precise individual, and he provided keen oversight to the building of the home. The Barton House was one of the first homes to be built on Michaux. When the house was completed, Michaux was not yet paved. Photo by Jill Blackburn.

Bell House

The Gerald and Christine Bell House, at 1707 Michaux, was built by C. S. Witt in 1969. The Bells admired the design work of Louis Sumner Winn, Jr. and arranged a time to meet with Winn at his home. They arrived to find Winn wearing his bathing suit and cleaning a shotgun. Despite this less than conventional introduction, the Bells wanted Winn to be their architect. They particularly appreciated his designs that emphasized the connections between the interior and exterior of his homes and his use of corner windows. Landscaping for the Bell House was designed by Dick Bell (no relation). The original screen porch was enclosed in glass in 2000. Photo by Heather Wagner.

Bowles House

Victor P. and Doris Bowles purchased the property at 1712 Michaux Road in 1967. Victor worked as the Director of Budget and Finance at the University of North Carolina at Chapel Hill. In 1968, C.S. Witt designed and built this mid-century modernist home. Photo by Jim Pearce.

Byrd House

The Robert and Pat Byrd House at 404 North Elliott Road was built in 1968 by JP Goforth. The home was one of Goforth's earliest building projects from a modernist house plan. Robert Byrd was a professor and then Dean of the School of Law at the University of

North Carolina at Chapel Hill. The wide, low-roofed front-gabled house has the bold, overhanging roofline of the Bay Area California style. But its façade is more open, with tall windows and transoms flanking the central recessed entrance. There is also a daylight basement. (Source Bob Byrd, interviewed by Tom Heffner, August, 2005) Photo by Lucy Pittman.

Choi House

In 1972, Sang-il and Etsuyo Choi built their home at 1714 Michaux Road. JP Goforth built the house for the Choi's. The home is nestled in a natural setting and features the modernist flat roof. Photo by Jill Blackburn.

Cogswell House

Architect Arthur Cogswell designed his home at 308 North Elliott Road. The home won an award from the North Carolina Chapter of the AIA and is considered one of Cogswell's most inspired residential designs. The home was also one of the first homes in the state to be built around an interior courtyard pool. Cogswell purchased the property from Dr. Jack and Louise Behrman in 1965. The design and building of the house was completed during 1969-1970. There are interior and exterior brick floors, simple geometric forms, large, white, un-textured surfaces, expansive areas of glass and the general use of steel and reinforced concrete construction. Cogswell wanted a home that was not of "stick" construction and on a flat lot. The house is sited on a low, flat knoll, with a traditional Chapel Hill stone retaining wall, stone steps and sidewalk leading to the modern one-story, flat-roofed steel frame house with white walls. One bay of the six-bay-wide house is a recessed entrance. The only sources of light on the façade are slender windows in a band beneath the eaves. Above the right two bays, the glazed upper level of the two-story living room rises above the rest of the house. The stark severity of the exterior is in contrast to an oasis on the inside with a one-room-deep square surrounding a courtyard containing a terrace and large heated swimming pool. A continuous wall of sliding glass doors separates the living and dining areas and the corridor along the bedrooms from the courtyard. Gil Thurlow was the landscape architect. Photo courtesy of NC Modernist Houses.

Conway-Thompson House

Eugenia (Cece) Conway and Tommy Thompson's House at 1720 Allard Road was designed and built by JP Goforth. Tommy Thompson was the original banjo player for the musical group, the Red Clay Ramblers. The Conway-Thompson's moved into the home in October 1973. Photo by Jill Blackburn.

Crounse House

The Crounse House at 1730 Allard Road was built for Marion and Robert G. Crounse in 1972. Dr. Crounse was a dermatologist at the University of North Carolina at Chapel Hill, School of Medicine. The home was designed by Ann Bickett Parker Stevens and built by Jack Stevens. Photo by Chase Hanes.

Eastman House

The Sidney Louis Eastman House at 1710 Michaux Road was built in 1968 by JP Goforth with design oversight by J. Knox Tate, IV.
Photo by Jill Blackburn.

Falk House

The Falk House at 1711 Allard Road was built in 1972 for Jeanette and David Falk. JP Goforth was the designer and builder. The home was styled after a Deck House. Jeanette Falk was the founder of the Children's Store in Chapel Hill. Photo by Jill Blackburn.

Fire Station Three

Fire Station Three at the corner of North Elliott Road and East Franklin Street was built by Delta Construction. The property, deeded in Coker Hills, was purchased by Robert and Catherine

Cox and then sold to the Town of Chapel Hill. The fire station was designed by Cogswell/Hausler and received an Award of Merit from the North Carolina Chapter of the AIA in 1971. The primary architect for the project was Toby Savage. The jury commented on the unpretentious handling of the building and siting, and the architects made every effort, through treatment, to minimize its obtrusive effect in a residential neighborhood. The detailing is crisp and unusually careful. Gil Thurlow, a Professor of Landscape Architecture from North Carolina State University was commissioned by the Town of Chapel Hill to complete the landscape design. Photo by Jill Blackburn.

Goodwin House

The Frances Brantly Goodwin House at 406 Lyons Road was built in 1968. Goodwin moved to North Carolina from Santa Fe, New Mexico where her home had been designed by Frank Welch, a noted Texas modernist architect. Taking ideas from that home, she created a new house with additional inspirations from a modernist plan. Carolina Builders provided and installed the original Pella windows. Ellen Weinstein designed the addition to the house which was completed in 2004. The hardscape designer was Dick Henry. Photo by Janet Kagan.

Hanst House

The Hanst House at 1732 Allard Road was built for Constance D. and Phillip Lincoln Hanst. The house was built by L. H. Rhew. Dr. Hanst was a pioneer of air pollution research using infrared spectroscopy. He loved opera and growing vegetables in his garden.

Photo by Chase Hanes.

Hill House

Dr. David Hill, Professor of Engineering at Duke University, purchased the land at 205 Wood Circle from Coker College. Arthur Cogswell designed the modernist residence during his first year in solo practice. Dr. Hill served as the General Contractor. The house was completed in 1963 with a unique barrel-vaulted roof design which required concrete roof segments to be built on site using wooden forms. A large crane was on site to lift the heavy concrete segments onto the top of the house. The series of vaults, supported by steel posts in the center of the house, extend out as a cantilevered roof to either side of the structure. The house is unique in that the barrel-vaulted concrete roof resembles the tops of a series of gothic arches. Bill Hunt was the landscape designer. Photo courtesy of NC Modernist Houses.

Hinsdale House

Charles Edward (Ed) and Ann Lee Hinsdale purchased property at 1405 Michaux Road. Their home was built in 1962. The architect was Arthur Norman Tuttle, Jr. AIA, and the builder was Van Thomas of Siler City. Ed Hinsdale worked for the University of North Carolina at Chapel Hill, School of Government. Photo by NC Modernist Houses.

Hubbard House

In 1967, Paul and Sylvia Hubbard purchased the property at 1710 Audubon. JP Goforth built the home based on a design by L.M. Brunier and Associates of Portland, Oregon with extensive modifications by the owners. A beautiful view of the wooded hillside is enjoyed from the main rooms of the house which are on the upper level. The interior has wood-paneled walls in most rooms and a Crab Orchard Stone floor in the entry way. There are fireplaces in the upstairs living room and in the downstairs playroom. Photo by Jim Pearce.

Kessing House

The Jonas and Alice Kessing House at 401 North Elliott Road was built in 1962. The home was a prefab house designed by Richard Wright. The Kessing Pool at the University of North Carolina at Chapel Hill, outside of Woolen Gym, was named for Jonas's father. According to Alice Kessing, they hired Oliver Spainhour to assemble and build their home. In 1964, they added another room. In 1973, the house was sold to Sam Longiotti, the developer for the South Square Mall in Durham, North Carolina and the Siena Hotel in Chapel Hill, North Carolina, although he never resided in the home. More extensive renovations were completed in 2011 by owners, Wai Lee Lui and Johannes H. Hoerler. The design was provided by Vinny Petrarca and built by David Ballard Construction. Landscape design by Francis Landscaping. Photo courtesy of NC Modernist Houses.

Koch House

The William J. and Dorothy C. Koch House, 401 Clayton Road, was designed by Arthur Cogswell and was built in 1964. Cogswell designed the single story, flat-roofed house for the Koch's using the "International Style" associated with Cogswell's mentor, George Matsumoto. This bold modernist house, sits on a large piece of property abutting a protected greenway. The International Style house is a platform, cantilevered over a concrete block foundation, with a carport and a covered corridor forming the street façade. The carport wall is a tall, vertically-louvered screen which conceals parked vehicles. The house faces the rear of the property where transparent walls open to a deck and a pond in the back yard. Joseph Nassif, who worked with Cogswell/Hausler, provided the construction oversight of the home. Cogswell won a Merit Award for this home from the North Carolina Chapter of the American Institute of Architects in 1965. Professor William J. Koch was a Professor of Botany, Biology and Mycology at the University of North Carolina at Chapel Hill, and his wife Dorothy was a writer of children books. Thomas Kenan purchased the property from the Koch's in 1974. Photo courtesy NC Modernist Houses.

Lindahl House

The Roy and Gwen Lindahl House at 305 Clayton Road was commissioned in 1964 and built in 1965. Dr. Lindahl was a faculty member in the School of Dentistry, University of North Carolina at Chapel Hill. The architect was Harwell Hamilton Harris, and the builder was F.E. Osborne from Wake Forest. A remodel was done in 2005 by owners Jason and Teresa Wilson. Bill Waddell was the architect. Photo by Bill Waddell.

Locher House

Walter and Gretchen Locher retired to Chapel Hill after a career in the oil industry. The house at 1713 Audubon was built by JP Goforth in 1969. Photos by Heather Wagner.

Monroe House

Built in 1970 at 404 Lyons Road, the house was designed by architect Ann Bickett Parker Stevens and built by Jack Stevens for John T. and Jane K. Monroe, Jr. John Harris of North Carolina State University was consulted on the landscape design. In 1977, the owners added a master bedroom suite. Original owner, Jane Monroe claimed the home had the first whirlpool tub in Chapel Hill. In 1984, new owners Joseph O. and Alice Moore finished the basement and added two rooms. The home was sold again in 2003 to Peter C. Gordon and Janet A. Chambers who have done further renovations and expansions. Photo by Heather Wagner.

Perry House

On the corner of Audubon and North Elliott, at 311 North Elliott Road, the Perry House was built as a parsonage by Holy Trinity Lutheran Church of Chapel Hill for their Pastor Frank Perry, his wife, Martha, and their family. This was the first church parsonage built at a distance from the church proper on Rosemary Street in Chapel Hill. Louis Sumner Winn, Jr. was the architect for the house, and the builder was Lea and Fearrington from Mebane, North Carolina. Years later, Holy Trinity sold this property. Photo by Chase Hanes.

Philas House

Peter G. and Ida Philas purchased the land at 1704 Curtis Road. Professor Philas was a faculty member in the English Department at the University of North Carolina at Chapel Hill. The home was designed by Arthur Cogswell and Warner Hausler. Hausler's designs were known for the slanted yet low slope, flat roofs. Joe Nassif of Cogswell/Hausler provided the bid and construction management. The house was completed in 1968, and the builder to the best of recall was Van Thomas, Siler City, North Carolina. Photo by Lucy Pittman.

Pickett House

Oscar A. and Fay E. Pickett, Jr. purchased the property located at 404 Clayton Road in 1960. The home was designed by Arthur Cogswell and built by Edward N. Mann, Sr. in 1963. Photo by NC Modernist Houses.

Prothro House

James W. and Mary Frances Prothro purchased land at 306 North Elliott in 1961 from Dr. Totten and Coker College. The Prothros moved to Chapel Hill in 1960 with their three daughters when Dr. Prothro accepted a position in the Department of Political Science at the University of North Carolina at Chapel Hill. The architect was Arthur Cogswell, and the builder was Edward N. Mann, Sr. The house was completed in 1962. In 1985, the home was sold to Dr. Martin and Barbara Rodbell. Barbara Rodbell lost her family in Auschwitz and survived the war in the Dutch underground. In 1994, Martin Rodbell received the Nobel Prize in Physiology and Medicine for the discovery of the G-proteins. Photo by Dail Dixon.

Rashkis House

Melvin "Mel" and Zora Rashkis purchased land at 415 Clayton Road from Coker College in 1963. Mel owned Rashkis and Associates Realty, at one time the largest real estate firm in Chapel Hill. Zora was a legendary public school teacher and Rashkis Elementary School in Meadowmont is named in their honor. The Rashkis House, completed in 1967, was a Donald Scholz home with the signature design of vaulted ceilings and beams. The house was completed in 1967 by Edward N. Mann, Sr. The home was renovated in 2012 with Ron Wilde as the architect and builder David Parker of Riverbank Custom Homes. Photo by NC Modernist Houses.

Rice House

In 1962, Oscar Knefler and Hope Sherfy Rice purchased the land from Coker College and built their home at 311 Clayton Road. The home was designed by Arthur Cogswell and built by Carl Ellington. The Rice house was one of the first homes to be built on Clayton Road. Dr. Oscar Rice (1903-1978) was a leader in the development of physical chemistry. For 42 years, he was a faculty member and Kenan Professor of Chemistry at the University of North Carolina at Chapel Hill. He was considered the most distinguished chemist to ever live in North Carolina. Photo by Julie Hollenbeck.

Royal House

Dr. Billy Williamson and Lil Royal purchased the land at 1703 Allard Road in 1964. The home was designed by Arthur Cogswell. During the years of 1966 to 1967, Roy McRee Spratt built the home. The supervising architect was James (Jim) Posey. Photo by Chase Hanes.

Rugen House

In 1984, Carolyn and Robert Rugen purchased the land at 1502 Velma from JP Goforth of Security Builders. The land was originally purchased in 1961 from Coker College and held by previous owners. Gary Giles was the architect, and the builder was Metz and Dehart. In 1989, a pool was added to the home. The original landscape designer was Linda Murray and later, Mary Jane Baker.
Photo by Chase Hanes.

Scott House

The Scott House at 1711 Audubon is the fruition of JP Goforth's design plans. Goforth built the home for Tom and Hattie Scott around 1970. The couple sold the home in 1986. Christian Arandel and Leila Hessini purchased the home in 2002. To better suit the needs of the family, Christian and Leila decided to renovate the home while respecting the original architectural design. Their renovation goals included respect for the architectural integrity of the house, to ensure environmental friendliness and comfort, the use of local materials and a design with fluid boundaries between the indoor and outdoor spaces. The architect for the design was Charles Holden of Oxide Architecture, Raleigh, North Carolina, and the renovation began in 2008. The landscape designer was Katherine Gill from Tributary Landscaping in Durham, North Carolina. Photo by Chase Hanes.

Sears House

The Bion and Mary Sears House at 1728 Allard Road was built in 1973 by David Lee Curl of Orange Builders. Elizabeth Bobbitt Lee of Lumberton, North Carolina was the architect. The property was originally purchased in 1966 by Quentin and Marjorie W. Lindsey. In 1972, the land was sold to the Sears and was one of the last unbuilt lots in Coker Hills. Mr. Sears was an alumnus of the University of North Carolina at Chapel Hill and a retired banker from Whiteville, North Carolina. Prior to their purchase, the Sears traveled to Asia and wanted to have a home with an Asian design. The interior and exterior of the home captures this aesthetic, including meditative Asian gardens.

Stehman Trillium House

The Stehman House at 407 Clayton Road was built by Carlyle John "Lyle" and Ursula Hampel Stehman in 1962. The home was designed by the Stehmans, and it is believed Lyle was the General Contractor. The home was designed with a large recreation room where square dances and card socials were frequently held. The Stehmans loved the woodland setting and the abundant wildflowers, including Trillium plants. The Stehmans sold their home in 1965, when Lyle was transferred to New York City by his company.

Photo by Heather Wagner.

Stehman White Oak House

The Stehmans were the original owners and designers of 409 Clayton Road. The property was purchased from Dr. Totten and Coker College by Lyle Stehman as a birthday present to his wife, Ursula. Ursula was very fond of the White Oaks on the land. When the Stehmans returned to Chapel Hill, they built their home in 1981. The design of the home allowed room for pianos, an organ, and open window space for observing the surrounding wildlife and woodland. The home was modified several times during the permit process. The Stehmans kept records of the home, including detailed drawings for the kitchen cabinets, installation instructions and even receipts. Don Higgs was the builder. Years later, Higgs enclosed the back deck and built a walk way to the front door. Photo by Chase Hanes.

Stephenson House

In 1968, the Robert M. Stephenson Jr. House at 1726 Allard Road was built by David Curl of Orange Builders. The architect is not known. Former owners, the Prazmas, added a studio. Photo by Jill Blackburn.

Stuart House

In 1971, the Stuart House at 417 Clayton Road was built by local area builder, L.H. Rhew, for George and Gene Stuart. George Stuart received his doctorate degree in Anthropology from the University of North Carolina at Chapel Hill. Dr. Stuart went on to become a staff archaeologist at the National Geographic Society and an authority on Mesoamerican sites. In 1990, Residential Services Inc. purchased the home. The home has been a "gold standard" in the successful integration of a group home into a residential neighborhood. Photo by Chase Hanes.

Townend House

In 1966, Cogswell/Hausler designed the house at 411 Clayton Road for Marion Townend. The elegant design includes a roof rising to the top of a four-sided pyramid, whose peak is a large skylight. The skylight is a ceiling for the living room, and the light is diffused into the surrounding rooms, changing their character as the sun moves across the sky. Three corners contain bedroom suites; the fourth contains the kitchen and service areas. Rooms can be opened to the center area by walls of sliding doors. The interior includes terrazzo floors, walls of pickled cypress and a massive stone wall that extends from the outside to form one wall of the entrance foyer and one wall of the living room. Photo by Lucy Pittman.

Warren House

Marsha and David Warren purchased the land at 408 Lyons Road from AC Robbins, a local realtor. In 1972-73, the Warrens built their home to duplicate their previously-owned deck home in New England. Robert (Bob) Bacon of BoMar Construction designed and built the home for the Warrens, using a modified deck house plan. The construction supervisor was Terry Lathrop. The home has interior ceilings of pine planking. In 1978, BoMar Construction built the accessory cottage. Dr. Warren was a faculty member at the Duke University School of Law. Photo by Chase Hanes.

Watkins House

The Julia Watkins House at 1708 Curtis Road was completed in 1966, designed by Brian Shawcroft and built by C.S. Witt. Julia Watkins was a faculty member and family nurse practitioner at the University of North Carolina at Chapel Hill School of Public Health. In her garden, she was known to grow okra and roses. Photo by NC Modernist.

Whittier House

In 1969, Anne Bickett Parker Stevens and her husband, Jack Stevens, designed and constructed the home at 402 Lyons Road. When the house was completed there was an economic downturn, and they were not able to sell the home. In 1972, the home was sold to Mary Avery Whittier. The house came with hundreds of building and material details recorded by Anne Stevens. In 1989, Mary Whittier completed an extensive remodel and addition, which included an indoor pool and fifty-eight skylights strategically placed to bring in the sun and stars. Anne Bickett Stevens was the architect for the renovation and the builder was Scott Jewell. During that time, an artesian well was dug, hitting 85 gpm of water at a depth of 25 feet. The house is a blend of art and architecture, vaulted tongue and groove ceilings dotted with skylights and custom wrought iron interior details by Ruffin Hobbs. There is elevator access from the lower level to the main area. Bruce McDowell Maggs purchased the home in 2007 and completed a renovation in 2014. The architect was Leonard J. Vogel of Vogel Residential Designs, and the builder was Bill Moneypenny. Photo by Brian Whittier.

Vickery House

Dr. Walter Neal Vickery was recruited by the University of North Carolina at Chapel Hill to establish the Department of Slavic Languages and Literature. Dr. Vickery served as the Department's founding chair. In 1969, Dr. Vickery purchased land at 1506 Velma, and JP Goforth built the home with plans from a similar home in Colorado. The McDonalds purchased the home in 2011 and completed an extensive redesign. The architect was John William (Bill) Waddell of Distinctive Architecture, and the builder was L.E. Meyers of Durham, North Carolina. Photo by Jill Blackburn.

Traditional Homes in Coker Hills

Building your own house is a primal urge, one of those universal genetic drives, like the need to provide for your family. — Kevin McCloud

I try to create homes, not houses.— Louis Kahn

Coker Hills is fortunate to have a blend of modernist and traditional style homes. Dr. Totten and Coker College created an approval process for the design and building of each new home.

The process provided for the neighborhood to include diverse styles and designs.

Like modernist homes, traditional homes were built to accommodate a way of life. In Coker Hills, some traditional homes are ranch style, which originated in California in the mid-1930s, inspired by the one-story southwest adobe buildings. There are also split-level ranch designs and two-story traditional homes in classical, colonial or Cape Cod designs. The split-level ranch is typically arranged with three types of interior space: a formal living and dining room, a casual family room utilized as a play or entertainment area and bedrooms typically located on the top floor. Many of the exteriors on these homes are brick or siding (usually cedar siding) or a combination of brick and siding. Traditional homes are known for their symmetrical style with a combination of classical detail such as paneled front doors, sidelights, shutters, gable ends, symmetrically placed double hung windows, hallway or entry, brick fireplace and covered or uncovered porches. Many traditional homes also include attached garages. The landscaping tends to be formal with brick walkways and/or low stone walls.

The following are some of the traditional homes in Coker Hills.

Allen House

The Allen House at 411 Lyons Road was built by L. H. Rhew of Durham, North Carolina. The original owners were Don Lee and Martha Allen. Dr. Allen was born in Burlington, North Carolina and was a graduate, professor, and associate dean at the University of North Carolina at Chapel Hill School of Dentistry before becoming dean at the University of Florida, College of Dentistry. An addition was completed in 2001 by Sankey Blanton and Susan Swanson. The architect was J. Knox Tate, IV, and the builder was Isenhour Enterprises. Photo by Chase Hanes.

Behrman House

Jack and Louise Behrman built their home at 1702 Audubon Road in 1965. Prior to living in Chapel Hill, they lived in Washington, D.C., where Jack worked for the Department of Commerce. He returned to Chapel Hill to accept a faculty position at the School of Business at the University of North Carolina at Chapel Hill. L. H. Rhew designed and built the home. When they purchased the property, Audubon was not yet paved. The Behrmans recalled that there were many trees on the land when they purchased the property, and there appeared to be what looked like a wagon trail along Audubon. Photo by Chase Hanes.

Bouldin House

Dr. Tom and Betty Bouldin purchased the land at 202 North Elliott Road in 1978 from Phil Hirsch, a professor at the University of North Carolina at Chapel Hill. JP Goforth and the Security Building Company built the home. Dr. Bouldin is a pathologist in the School of Medicine, University of North Carolina at Chapel Hill.

Photo by Chase Hanes.

Breslin House

Dr. Marianne Breslin was born in Bad Harzburg, Germany, and she graduated from the Medical Academy of Dusseldorf in 1946. She completed her residency in internal medicine. In 1951, under the Marshall Plan, she was awarded a U.S. government fellowship to continue her training at Presbyterian Hospital in New York City. In 1952, she came to Chapel Hill with her husband, Lou Breslin, who passed away five years later. Dr. Breslin completed her psychiatric training at the University of North Carolina at Chapel Hill and served as a faculty member at the university and at Duke University Medical School. In 1964, Dr. Breslin purchased the property at 1704 Michaux Road for $8000. Dr. Breslin was proud of her Coker Hills purchase, because in the 1960s it was difficult for a widow to purchase property. The architect for her home was Rudolph A. Matern, who prepared the plans, and Herman B. Lloyd was the builder. The home was completed in 1965. Photo by Jill Blackburn.

Clement House

Dr. John and Sylvia Clement moved to Chapel Hill from Ohio when John's company, Chemstrand, became one of the first companies to locate in Research Triangle Park, North Carolina. Joe Hakan prepared the blueprints for the home at 1603 Curtis Road. The purchase price for the property was $5,500, and the building cost was $26,000. Dr. Totten showed them every square inch of the property which was heavily wooded. Dr. Totten shared his knowledge about the various shrubs and trees on the property. The home was built by one of the Massey brothers from Burlington, North Carolina in 1962. Sylvia Clement said that when they built their home, Research Triangle Park had just opened resulting in a housing boom, leaving custom builders in short supply. Photo by Jill Blackburn.

Gastineau House

The Gastineau House at 409 Lyons Road was built for John William and Nova Jeanne Gastineau. Architect Merle Dixon collaborated with builder Dennis Howell to complete the home. Morris King was the landscape architect. Photo by Chase Hanes.

Glenn House

The home at 1705 Michaux Road was built for Willie L. and Nancy G. Glenn in 1968. The couple purchased the lot from Richard A. "Buddy" Birgel. Mr. Glenn worked for and was part owner of the

Triangle Brick Company, who made the brick for his home. Larry Ball was the residential home designer, and he worked closely with the builder, Odis Johnson of Hillsborough, North Carolina. Photo by Willie Glenn.

Hagadorn House

The Irvine R. Hagadorn House at 405 Lyons Road was built from 1970-1971 by JP Goforth with plans by Richard Pollman and Irving Palmquist, AIA. The Hagadorn family moved into the home in 1971 and sold the home in 1976. Dr. Hagadorn was the Chair of the Department of Zoology at the University of North Carolina at Chapel Hill. His investigations of leech endocrinology were pioneering and had implication for basic neuroendocrinology. The I.R. Hagadorn Award is given each year to an outstanding rising senior biology major at the university. An addition to the home was completed in 1993 by the Blackburns in consultation with architect Ellen Weinstein. Photo by Jill Blackburn.

E.C. Leonard House

Coker College deeded this property at 1703 Curtis Road to E.C. and Murlie Hinds Leonard in 1962. The Leonards were given the property in appreciation for all the work E. C. had done over the years to help Dr. Totten and Coker College with land surveys and engineering work. The Leonards designed the home. E.C. lived in the house for a short time before passing away. Murlie remained in the home for some years as a widow. Dr. Joe and Evelyn Grisham purchased the home from Mrs. Leonard. The Grisham's converted the sleeping porch into a sunroom. According to Mrs. Grisham, Mrs. Leonard loved the color pink and some of her bed frames were pink as well as the kitchen counter. The builder was Donnon Building. Photo by Jill Blackburn.

Maher House

The Phillip V. and Ruth G. Maher House at 417 Lyons Road was built in 1969. Herbert Hahn built several custom traditional style homes in Chapel Hill. This was the only custom home Hahn built in Coker Hills. Photo by Jill Blackburn.

Masson House

James and Barbara Masson purchased the land at 309 North Elliott Road. The Masson House was one of the first homes built in Coker Hills and was completed in 1961. The home is a traditional brick Cape Cod style. There is a similarly-designed home in Lake Forest at 2017 N. Lakeshore. The builder was H. Vernon Massey of Burlington, North Carolina. Photo by Chase Hanes.

Nelson House

Bruce Crumpton built this home at 410 Lyons Road, and in 1972 the home was featured in the Fall Chapel Hill Parade of Homes. Dr. William (Bill) and Susan Nelson purchased the home in 1973. Photo by Chase Hanes.

Summer House

In 1963, George K. and Betsy Summer purchased the land at 300 North Elliott Road. Their home was completed in 1966. The architect was James Lorn "J.L" Beam, Jr., and the builder was Herman Lloyd. Dr. Summer, a University of North Carolina at Chapel Hill graduate, later became Professor Emeritus of Biochemistry and Pediatrics at the University. Photo by Jill Blackburn.

Tillman House

The Tillman House at 209 Wood Circle was built for Dr. Rollie and Mary Windley Tillman. Dr. Tillman was a faculty member at the

School of Business, University of North Carolina at Chapel Hill and served for some years as the Vice Chancellor for University Relations. Tillman remembered walking with Dr. Totten, in 1961, from North Elliott Road to Wood Circle. Dr. Totten was a delightful person, eager to share his knowledge of plants and point out the trees worthy of being saved. Dr. Totten also provided suggestions for the optimal siting of the home. The Tillman house was built in 1961, and the builder, who could not be identified, was from the Hope Valley area. Rollie remembers the builder as being slow and careful. When the basement was poured, the builder waited weeks for the concrete to settle. North Elliott Road was newly paved at the time. Photo by Chase Hanes.

Ward House

The Ward House at 1504 Michaux Road was built in 1962 for Ira and Caroline Ward. Ira was a graduate of the School of Business, University of North Carolina at Chapel Hill, and later became President and Executive Officer of Orange Savings and Loan. The draftsman was Archie Davis of Weaver Dairy Road, Chapel Hill. Ira Ward's brother, Jasper (JP) Ward, was the builder. Photo by Chase Hanes.

Wysor House

Ida Lee Lauck and William Geoffrey "Bud" Wysor, Jr. purchased the land at 304 North Elliott Road from Dr. Totten and Coker College in 1963. The architect for their home was William Van Easton Sprinkle, and the builder was Lindsey Luther Fogelman. Dr. Wysor was a gastroenterologist, who graduated with a B.A. and M.D. from the University of Virginia. He became an Associate Professor of Medicine at the University of North Carolina at Chapel Hill before entering private practice with the Durham Internal Medicine Associates. Photo by Jill Blackburn.

5//The Coker Hills Legacy

The impersonal hand of government can never replace the helping hand of a neighbor. — Hubert H. Humphrey

What should young people do with their lives today? Many things obviously. But the most daring thing is to create stable communities in which the terrible disease of loneliness can be cured. — Kurt Vonnegut

Beyond the natural environment, architectural designs, and construction of homes is the Coker Hills legacy. This is a legacy not of monetary wealth, but of stories, memories and lasting friendships within the neighborhood. While gathering information for this book, conversations about the neighborhood evoked fond memories of garden club members, playground gatherings, caring neighbors, shared dinners, and even recipes. For many decades Coker Hills has been a special place to call home.

The Henry Roland Totten Garden Club

Addie Williams Totten **Henry Roland Totten**
1890-1974*   1892-1974*

Garden clubs formed as early as 1891, and they inspired future

Photograph courtesy of the University of North Carolina Chapel Hill Herbarium

generations of gardeners. Today, the National Garden Club is the largest volunteer organization of its type in the world. All fifty states have their own state garden clubs. In fact, there are 5,000 local garden clubs in the United States and 300 international affiliate clubs with a total of nearly 190,000 members. Addie and Henry Roland Totten were leaders in the garden club movement in North Carolina. One of their first clubs was established in the Laurel Hill neighborhood in Chapel Hill. In 1961, they established the Coker Hills Garden Club. They encouraged new owners to join the Garden Club, and they gladly shared their knowledge of plants. The Tottens enjoyed talking to and educating new owners on the variety of North Carolina plants that would likely flourish in their yards or gardens. They made generous donations of seeds, seedlings, and cuttings from their personal garden. Many of the plants currently found in the neighborhood, like Ligustrum, Liriope, Vinca, Equisetum, Hemerocallis, Physostegia, and Coralberry likely began as gifts from the Tottens. Club members honored Dr. Totten's efforts and vision in developing the neighborhood by re-naming their club, the Henry Roland Totten Garden Club.

The purpose of the club was to study horticulture and to encourage home and community beautification. The club was not only a way for neighbors to meet each other, but it also provided an opportunity to become better educated about plants and landscaping. Members received newsletters that also included information from the North Carolina Botanical Garden. Monthly meetings were held in members' homes from September through May, and at other times the club sponsored picnics and field trips. Some of the topics presented at meetings included: "Table Arrangements," "Container Gardening," "Soil Composition," "Shoka Style of Ikenobo Flower Arranging," "Early Spring Wildflowers," and "Our Garden Club and the Larger Community." The club also held potluck dinners to highlight club activities and accomplishments, and nonmembers from Coker Hills and Coker Hills West were invited to these functions. Club volunteer efforts included maintaining the neighborhood entrance signs and providing (when available) fresh flowers to the Chapel Hill Public Library, Estes Hills Elementary School, and Phillips Middle School.

The club organized clean-up campaigns and worked with the Town Council and public schools on community beautification projects. Plant sales and auctions were also conducted, with proceeds usually designated for the Totten Garden Center at the North Carolina Botanical Garden. By 1975, the club was providing holiday decorations for the waiting rooms at UNC Hospitals (then known as Memorial Hospital).

In a 1979 Garden Club Newsletter, President Isabel Fowler wrote, "I am looking forward to our garden club year ahead. You have been wonderful in your acceptance of responsibilities, all offices and committee jobs are filled and many members are already at work." In the September 1980 Garden Club Newsletter, President Fowler wrote, "I think you will all agree things are back in full swing in Chapel Hill, but the town is looking a little messy. Let's do what we can to pick up on the streets in our neighborhood and make it neater. In this hot, dry weather, it's hard to keep the waysides green, but maybe with a little effort, we can keep them green and clean." The president also congratulated two members who entered flower arrangements in the Community Rose Show. Anne Hinsdale won the first-place ribbon and Mary Kay Bozemski the third-place ribbon.

On March 17, 1977, The Henry Roland Totten Garden Club, in cooperation with the North Carolina Botanical Garden, presented a tribute to Dr. and Mrs. Totten. The tribute was entitled, "The Tottens: Recollections of Colleagues and Friends," and it was held at the Totten Garden Center at the North Carolina Botanical Garden. Former students of Dr. Totten spoke, including William Lanier Hunt, a writer and lecturer on horticulture. Lydia "Pete" Hobson, an original Coker Hills owner and a charter member of the Henry Roland Totten Garden Club, also spoke. She concluded her remarks by noting that "As long as these varied woods continue to grow and the residents continue to meet in neighborly fellowship to work at preserving and creating beauty, so long will the influence of the Tottens continue to be in Coker Hills."

Over the years, membership in the Henry Roland Totten Garden Club began to decline, as members moved or passed away. The original owners benefitted from the accumulated knowledge of the garden club, but recent generations of owners felt they needed less gardening and landscaping assistance. On January 24, 1991, in honor of the thirtieth anniversary of the Club, an auction was held at the home of Zora and Mel Rashkis at 415 Clayton Road. The auction celebrated thirty years of the garden club's community service, beautification, and neighborhood friendship. The proceeds from the auction provided for a donation to the Totten Garden Center and to support the purchase of new entrance signs for the neighborhood. All past and current members were invited for what was to be the final club gathering. The list of invitees included:

Julie Andresen McClintock, Louise Behrman, Priscilla Bevin, Nancy Bless, Mary Kay Bozemski, Marion Brinson, Mary Carroll, Elizabeth Carter (the club's first president), Betty Chase, Julia Clark, Sylvia Clements, Betty Davis, Elizabeth Edmands, Gloria Ernest, Isabel Fowler, Millie Gerard, Evelyn Grisham, Helen Hawley, Diane Henry, Anne Hinsdale, Pete Hobson, Genie Jansen, Marge Jennings, Jane Kaufman, Patty Krebs, Jean LaCombe, Minerva Levin, Mitchel Lyman, Lillian Royal, Hope Rice, Charlotte Stanmeyer, Ursula Stehman, Jane Steele, Marian Stevenson, Barbara Stocking, Paula Smith, Ruth Swanson, Cheryl Tattle, Alberta Via, Carolyn Ward, Judy Watkins, Fran Weaver, Johnsie Wilkins, Lee Wysor, and Pearl Yohe.

Genie Jansen of 407 Clayton Road and former club president said, "Although the club was disbanded, we all have many happy memories and many beautifully landscaped properties in Coker Hills."

E.C. Leonard Playground

Murlie Hinds Leonard
1891–1981*

Edward Charles Leonard, Sr.
1889–1963*

Another legacy of Totten's early vision for the Coker Hills neighborhood was the establishment of a neighborhood playground. Dr. Totten thought that a playground, perhaps managed by the town, would be a nice addition to the neighborhood, and an amenity that town council members might look upon with favor. As the Coker Hills lots were surveyed and mapped, one parcel, Lot 26 at the corner of Clayton and Audubon Roads ended up as non-conforming, because it was smaller than the required lot size of 0.6 acres. In 1962, Lot 26 was officially des-

Photos courtesy of Earlham College

ignated for use as a playground, and ownership of the lot was transferred from Coker College to the playground association. The playground was named in honor of Edward Charles "E.C." Leonard, Sr. for his many years of service and effort to make the Coker Hills neighborhood a reality.

E.C. Leonard was born in Guilford County, North Carolina on March 17, 1889 to a Quaker family. Legend has it that the family was related to Edward R. Murrow, the early pioneer of radio and television broadcasting. In 1902, the family moved to Indiana, and in 1907, E.C. graduated from high school and attended Earlham College in Richmond, Indiana. During the summer of 1911, E.C. worked as a cook for the US Soil Survey in Indiana, and in 1913, he graduated from Earlham with a Bachelor of Science in Chemistry. His senior yearbook quote read, *"One science only will one genius fit, so vast is art, so narrow human wit."* After graduating from college, E.C. returned to the US Soil Survey, but this time he was sent to the Florida Everglades to work. He left that position in 1915 to become a public school teacher in Wilson, North Carolina.

E.C. met his future wife, Murlie Hinds of New Castle, Indiana, at Earlham, but it would be many years before they would marry. In Murlie's college yearbook her description read, *"The littlest girl in the class and she lisps. She is most charming."* It is likely that the writer of this remark had not realized that Murlie had contracted scarlet fever as a young girl, and as a result lost some of her hearing, leading to the development of a slight speech impediment. Murlie graduated from Earlham in 1915 with degrees in biology and German and became a teacher.

In 1925, E.C. and Murlie married and their first son, E.C. Jr., was born in 1927, and a second son, Colbert, followed in 1929.

The Leonard family lived in Alamance County during the

1930s. E.C. taught science at Burlington High School for many years and later became the principal of the school. During World War II, with a shortage of faculty at the university level, he was asked to teach physics at the University of North Carolina at Chapel Hill. The family moved to Chapel Hill, residing at 305 Cameron Avenue.

In researching Mr. Leonard's life, the Earlham Alumni Association noted his profession as a civil engineer. As such, he worked on many local developments, including Morgan Creek, Coker Hills, and other properties owned by Dr. Coker. As mentioned, Totten and Coker College were most appreciative of Leonard's efforts to develop the Coker Hills neighborhood. In appreciation for his service, they provided the Leonards with a Coker Hills lot of their choice. In 1961, the Leonards selected the lot at 1703 Curtis Road for their new home. When their home was completed, Curtis Road was still a dirt road and ended at their house. An original owner recalled visiting the Leonard's home and noted that when sitting on their side porch you could see all the way down to Eastwood Lake. The large pines that now block that view were young, short saplings at the time.

When the Leonards moved into their new home, their two sons were already young adults. Their older son, E.C. Jr. (Charles), was advancing through executive positions in various chemical companies while their younger son, Colbert, worked in advertising in New York City.

Mrs. Leonard was an avid reader, often checking out twenty or more books every time she went to the Chapel Hill Public Library. She was a talented seamstress and made uniforms for her son, Charles, while he attended the Citadel before transferring to the University of North Carolina at Chapel Hill. She also made clothing for neighbors. Neighbor Caroline Ward of 1504 Michaux Road recalled that Mrs. Leonard made an attractive red dress for her to wear to the 1964 New York World's Fair. She also made four matching shirts for the Waddell children at 408 North Elliott, who were also going to the World's Fair. She was like a family member or grandmother to many families in the neighborhood. She enjoyed sharing her recipes and dishes, especially her recipe for sesame flounder. Neighborhood children looked forward to visiting the Leonard house for Halloween. Murlie was known for handing out her delicious, warm homemade donuts for their treat. Gardening was another of her favorite past times, and each year she organized a neighborhood azalea sale. She would purchase a pallet of azaleas and sell them to neighbors at wholesale prices. To this day, some of these original plants beautify the neighborhood with their colorful blooms each spring.

Azaleas at 1603 Curtis Road
Photo by Jill Blackburn

E.C. Leonard passed away from a heart attack on February 23, 1963, shortly after moving into his new home. In his memory, the neighborhood playground was named in his honor. Murlie remained in the home for some time afterward, before moving into the Friends Home at Guilford, in Greensboro, North Carolina. In 1963, Murlie and her son Charles sent a note addressed to "Dear Friends of Coker Hills," which read in part: "When we think of you and what you have done, we will remember you with love, respect, and admiration. You opened your arms and hearts with compassion. We can never, never cease being grateful for such truly fine friends. You will always have a special place in our hearts." When Murlie died in 1982 in Guilford County, she remembered the E.C. Leonard Playground in her estate with a five hundred dollar bequest.

The secretary of state for North Carolina signed the Articles of Incorporation for the E.C. Leonard Playground on May 16, 1963. Under these articles, the playground became a nonprofit corporation under the laws of North Carolina. The corporation remains in perpetuity, with the stated purpose to organize, construct, build, maintain, and operate a playground, picnic area, and other recreational facilities for the benefit of its members in accordance with the provisions of the charter and by-laws adopted.

On October 21, 1971, Warren Via of 307 Clayton Road, Treasurer of the E.C. Leonard Playground Board, wrote to Members and Friends of the E.C. Leonard Playground "when the playground was given to us it was an eyesore-quite rocky and overgrown with a very large gulley and all the trimmings of poison ivy and poison oak thrown in. We had several workdays, and it is now used by the boys and girls of Coker Hills and some of their friends. One basketball goal was given by the Sertoma Club, and we need another one now for the coming season. Some scraping and filling needs to be done to make it really usable." For many years, the Chase family, whose property bordered the playground on Clayton Road, took care of the property and installed a basketball court.

Property taxes for the playground were originally paid from the annual dues and assessments paid by neighbors. Fortunately, in 1975, Victor Bowles, the original owner at 1712 Michaux, playground Board president, and the UNC Director of Budget and Finance filed for a non-profit tax exemption for the playground from Orange County. Although the initial application was denied, Mr. Bowles filed an appeal, and on August 6, 1975, the playground was granted tax-exempt status.

Over the years, the playground has been the site of many neighborhood gatherings, particularly the Coker Hills Annual Neighborhood Picnics. Residents socialized and children would play while hamburgers and hot dogs sizzled on grills. More recently, the Coker Hills Neighborhood Association provided BBQ and chicken along with beverages at this event, while neighbors provided sides and desserts. Members of the group home on Clayton Road always looked forward to attending.

Some years the neighborhood held an Ice Cream Social at the playground. For two consecutive years, the neighborhood won an Edy's Neighborhood Ice Cream contest. One year the win celebrated the 102nd birthday of Mrs. Florence Krebs who lived with her daughter, Patty, at 309 North Elliot Road. The next year the social welcomed Sankey Blanton of 411 Lyons Road home from a fourteen-month Army tour in Afghanistan.

By 2006, playground funds were declining, so on September 30 of that year, Patty Krebs organized a "Jumble Sale" to raise funds for the playground. Neighbors donated items and their time to make the sale a success. The sale raised slightly more than $1000 and was a wonderful way for neighbors to work together for a worthwhile cause. A second fundraiser, a plant sale, also organized by Patty, was held on May 26, 2007. Plants for sale were donated by neighbors and proceeds were used to improve the playground.

Walkway to the Public School

The well-trod blacktop walkway, from the intersection of North Elliot Road and Curtis Road up to Estes Hills Elementary School, was built on land donated to the Chapel Hill Public School System by Mr. Ed Tenney, who was given the parcel by Coker College. Mr. Tenney was an original owner at 305 North Elliot. In the early 2000s, eight schoolgirls would meet every morning at the stop sign by the path. They became known as the "Stop Sign Girls" and by middle school, the "Stop Sign Sisters." Over the years, countless children, parents and pets have walked this path to and from the schools and athletic fields. The pathway continues to provide safe access to the schools for the neighborhood.

Coker Hills Stop Sign Sisters
(Back Left-Right: Claire Williamson, Elizabeth Hart, Jennifer Blackburn, Leah Kagan Reznick, Kiersten Paul, Emily Branson, Erika Edwards, and Mary Claire Lachiewicz)

Photo by Dick Blackburn

Integration of a Group Home

In 1990, the home at 417 Clayton Road was sold to Residential Services Inc. (RSI), a nonprofit corporation providing services to adults with developmental disabilities. The organization was founded in 1974 as Orange County Group Homes. Later, the organization changed its name to RSI. In the late 1980s, RSI needed to find a few additional homes in Chapel Hill. Unlike some neighborhoods that reacted to a group home with fear and trepidation, Coker Hills welcomed the integration of the home into the neighborhood. For almost twenty-five years, the home has stood as a model of successful integration of a group home into an existing neighborhood. The home has peacefully coexisted with the neighborhood, and it has been well-managed and maintained by RSI. Neighbors have gotten to know the residents, and residents are invited to all neighborhood events.

The home is designed with shared living space and each resident has the responsibility for chores. Residents and staff are often seen walking to nearby stores, or just out enjoying the day. During the week residents have employment, either in Chapel Hill or at OE Enterprises, a sheltered workshop for vocational training in Hillsborough, North Carolina. RSI promotes happy and healthy living along with social responsibility and productivity for its residents.

Coker Hills Recipes

The word "recipe" comes from the Latin word, "recipere," meaning to take or receive. As new neighbors moved into Coker Hills, new neighbors became friends and sometimes became extended family. Sharing recipes became a reflection of this neighborly relationship, a way to create closer bonds and wonderful memories. In a recent meeting with some of the original owners in Coker Hills, participants spoke about dishes and meals they shared and some of their favorite neighborhood recipes.

Murlie Leonard's Homemade Doughnuts

While candy was a common treat for children in the neighborhood on Halloween night, Murlie Leonard was known for making delicious donuts.

3½ cups all-purpose flour	½ tsp. cinnamon	¾ cup milk
1 cup sugar	¼ tsp. nutmeg	2 eggs
3 tsp. baking powder	2 tbsp. butter	½ tsp. salt

Heat oil (2-4 inches deep) on high. Measure 1½ cups of flour and all remaining ingredients in a large mixing bowl. Blend at low speed, scraping the bowl constantly, and stirring in the remaining flour. Put the dough on a well-floured surface. Roll the dough around to lightly coat with flour. Roll dough 3/8 inches thick. Cut the dough with a floured doughnut cutter. With a wide spatula, slide the doughnuts into hot oil, turning them when they rise to the surface. Cook 2–3 minutes or until golden brown on both sides. Remove carefully from oil. Drain. Serve plain, sugared, or frosted. Makes 2 dozen doughnuts.

Murlie Leonard's Persimmon Pudding

Mrs. Leonard was known for making this desert, using fresh persimmons from the trees in the neighborhood. In this recipe, persimmon pulp is combined with eggs, sugar, flour, and butter and baked in the oven rather than steamed in a pudding mold.

½ tsp. baking soda
½ tsp. salt
2 tbsp. butter
2 eggs, beaten
1 cup persimmon pulp

3/4 cup sugar
1 cup sifted flour
½ tsp. lemon rind
1 cup milk

Sift together flour, salt, soda, and sugar. Add remaining ingredients. Mix well. Pour batter into greased and floured 8x8x2 inch baking dish. Bake at 350 degrees for 50 minutes or until done. Serve warm with whipped cream, hard sauce or lemon sauce. Serves 6.

Pearl Yohe's Hermits

Chris Waddell Nutter was one of the first homeowners in Coker Hills. She recalled Pearl Yohe's wonderful recipe that her children enjoyed. The Yohes lived at 413 North Elliott Road.

1½ cups butter	4½ cups flour
2 cups sugar	2 tsp. cinnamon
2 eggs	1½ tsp. ginger
½ cup dark molasses	1½ tsp. cloves
4 tsp. baking soda	1 cup raisins (if desired)
½ tsp. salt	

Mix butter, sugar, eggs, and dark molasses. Add all remaining ingredients to the first mixture. Add raisins last. Roll out like a sausage on a floured board – 1 inch in diameter. Place roll on a cookie sheet and squash slightly. Shake sugar on the rolls. Bake at 375 degrees for 9 minutes or until top is cracked. Remove from the oven and cool slightly before cutting into strips on an angle. Makes four logs on two cookie sheets. Another option: Instead of sprinkling with sugar, put a glaze on the roll while it is still warm. Glaze: Mix equal parts of confectioner's sugar and milk.

The Totten's Pickled String Beans

Neighbors remember being invited to the Totten's home in Laurel Hill for late summer gatherings. The Tottens served one of their favorite recipes using their garden-grown beans. Pickled string beans, also known as Dilly Beans, were popular in the South and were a means to preserve the summer legume. Serve as a snack, in a salad, or as a side dish.

16 oz. mason type jar	2 cloves fresh garlic - mashed
½ pound string beans	½ cup white vinegar
1 tsp. yellow mustard seeds	½ cup water
¼ tsp. whole peppercorns	Dash red pepper flakes
1 bay leaf	Sprigs of dill or dill weed

Place the string beans upright in the glass jar. Trim any ends that reach the top of the jar. Add dill sprigs. Combine all other ingredients in a saucepan and cook on the stove (for the modern version, cook in the microwave) until warm and blended. If using the microwave, cook for 90 seconds, stir, and then microwave for another 90 seconds. Pour the mixture into the jar leaving ½-inch space at the top. Screw on the lid. Let cool to room temperature.

Murlie Leonard's Sesame Flounder

Chris Waddell Nutter of 408 North Elliott Road shared this recipe and said, "Mrs. Leonard was our family's adopted grandmother. She adopted our family [the Waddell family], and we adopted her." This was one of her famous recipes.

¼ cup sesame seeds	2 cups soft white bread crumbs
1½ pounds fresh or frozen flounder	1/8 tsp. pepper
¾ tsp. salt	1/8 tsp. thyme
½ cup melted butter	

Brown sesame seeds on a baking sheet. If fish is frozen, allow to thaw. Arrange fish in a 3-quart casserole dish. Add a very small amount of water. Mix bread crumbs, sesame seeds, butter, salt, pepper, and thyme. Spread evenly over the fish and bake at 325 degrees for 30–40 minutes or until the fish flakes.

Recipe for an Outstanding Neighborhood

2 cups of kindness	2 cups friendship
2 cups of understanding	3 cups of forgiveness
5 tbsp. of hope	1 cup of caring
4 quarts of faith	1 barrel of laughter

Take kindness and friendship, mix thoroughly with caring. Blend this with understanding and forgiveness. Add hope and faith. Sprinkle abundantly with laughter. Pour into a neighborhood and bake in the sunshine. Serves an entire neighborhood forever.

6//Growing Up in Coker Hills

Growing up happens in a heartbeat. One day you are in diapers, the next you are gone, but the memories of childhood stay with you for the long haul. — The Wonder Years

For children growing up in the early days of Coker Hills, the neighborhood was a vast playground; a patchwork of undeveloped wooded areas, construction sites, and newly-built houses; each house holding the promise of potential playmates. Children roamed freely as far as bikes and legs could carry them. The day's end was signaled by parents ringing a bell, a system so common that neighborhood kids could easily distinguish the tone of one bell from another. For some, like Sophie Cogswell and her sister, Amanda, no bell was necessary. Sophie and Amanda were simply told to be home when the streetlights came on. As their father, Arthur, put it, the children of Coker Hills were raised with "benign neglect."[1]

Coker Hills was dominated by two broad, tree-lined roads, North Elliott and Clayton. Most yards retained their natural landscaping; with so much greenery, it was difficult to see the houses from the street. Since there were no sidewalks, kids traveled directly on the roads, but there was so little traffic this didn't present a problem. In fact, the favorite napping spot for the Cogswells' hound dog, Rebecca, was in the middle of North Elliott Road. She often slept there undisturbed for long periods of time.

---

[1] *With special appreciation to Susan Prothro Worley, author of this chapter, along with the following former residents of Coker Hills: Elizabeth Sophia Cogswell Baskin, Dale Evarts, John Floyd, Anne Geer, Sarah Geer, Bill Lassiter, Nancy Hinsdale Poole, David Summer, Juliann Tenney, and Skip Via.*

In those early days, most of the neighborhood families were headed by two parents, and the majority of women didn't work outside the home. Husbands had jobs at the university, in the recently-established Research Triangle Park, or elsewhere in the area. Inside the walls of these newly built houses, one could find examples of the usual dysfunctions that family life engenders. Outside, however, kids played happily, easily finding opportunities for companionship and fun.

In 1960, Carl Ellington built one of the first houses in the neighborhood at 307 Clayton Road. It would become home to the Via family. Skip Via was ten years old when his family moved in, and he remembers that the Jennings' home at 304 Clayton was one of the few finished houses on the street. North Elliott Road was not yet paved, and the entire neighborhood was dotted with construction sites. As houses were completed and owners moved in, it quickly became apparent that Coker Hills would be a neighborhood full of children. Many families like the Lindahls, Gills, Cogswells, Kessings, Taylors, Lassiters, Massons, Gleasons, Royals, Wysors, Hinsdales, and Kochs had at least two children, so no one ever lacked for playmates.

Skip Via remembers Coker Hills' parents hoping that the land at the corner of Clayton and Audubon would become a neighborhood playground or park. Their hopes became a reality in 1963 but not without countless hours of volunteer efforts. What today is the E. C. Leonard Playground was then an empty lot, filled with construction debris, brambles, and honeysuckle. Neighbors willingly pitched in to clear the brush and debris and piled it high in the center of the property. At the end of the cleanup, a huge bonfire reduced the pile to ashes. Trucks hauled in fill dirt to bring the property elevation up to street level. Volunteers planted grass, shrubs, and trees and took turns mowing the lawn that eventually appeared. It is likely that the town donated the water faucet at the playground, but it was something of a coup to get it installed. The playground became the scene of many epic football games involving neighborhood boys and, occasionally, a girl or two.

Although neighborhood parents went to much trouble to create a playground for their children, it was an unprepossessing bit of pavement at the cul-de-sac at the top of Clayton Road that became the favorite gathering place for the children. No child was familiar with the term "cul-de-sac" in the early 1960s, so the area was known simply as "The Circle." Kids gravitated to The Circle after school and on weekends, often playing afternoon and evening kickball and softball games as the weather allowed. But just as frequently to simply hang out, the way children do when left to their own devices. Skip's dad, Warren Via, painted bases around the perimeter of The Circle, and the manhole cover in the center served as the pitcher's "mound." Skip recalls, "The worst position to play was first base, since a missed throw to first would result in a long chase down the hill to retrieve the ball."

When not on The Circle, kids found driveways with basketball hoops, where they shot baskets and imagined themselves to be Tar Heel standouts like Billy Cunningham, Larry Miller, or Charlie Scott. The Taylors on Allard Road had an amazing basketball goal complete with supporting guy-wires, and the Vias were much appreciated for allowing children to shoot hoops at their place even when they weren't home. In the mid-1960s, a nationwide skateboarding craze reached the neighborhood. There were enough hills to offer plenty of opportunities for skinned knees and sprained wrists as kids careened down driveways along Allard and Clayton Roads without helmets or protection of any kind. Yet somehow, these kids survived childhood.

In the early 1960s, Michaux, Allard, and Audubon Roads were short, unconnected stubs off North Elliott Road. From the backyards of houses on the east side of North Elliott down to Lake Forest, there was nothing but woods and meadows. A trail that ran down the hill through the woods made for thrilling bike rides (mountain biking before its time), though it was a tough climb back up to North Elliott. Blackberry bushes in the meadow yielded berries for cobblers. At the bottom of the hill, tadpole pools required happy investigation. After Michaux was extended to connect with Allard and Audubon, road construction left giant mounds of yellow clay, behind which kids would hide and throw big clods of dirt at each other, all in good fun.

With so many children in the neighborhood, it was easy to round up enough participants for games that required teams. Summer evenings saw many an entertaining game of Kick the Can on Allard and Audubon. The undeveloped woods west of Michaux (where the Chapel Hill Public Library now stands) were an ideal place for forts and hideouts. Kids divided up into teams, marking their forts with flags before scouting enemy forts to steal their flags.

In those early days, there were still farmhouses scattered about the neighborhood as well as other occasional reminders of Coker Hills' rural past. Dale Evarts recalls the remains of an old farm road that paralleled North Elliott Road and went by the front porch of his house at 415 North Elliott. The Evarts's backyard had short pine trees coming out of furrows that had once been part of a farm field. Juliann Tenney, who also lived on North Elliott Road, remembers a man with a plot of land near Franklin Street, close to what is now Sunrise Biscuit Kitchen, who grew the best corn she ever ate. When Sophie Cogswell's home at 308 North Elliott was under construction in the late 1960s, a family stopped by while Sophie and her parents were visiting the construction site. The family had lived on a farm somewhere in the neighborhood, and for years they had come to collect holly from a huge tree in the Cogswell's yard so they could make Christmas wreaths to sell. The Cogswells told them they were welcome to continue to come as long as they liked, but the family was never seen again.

The lake in Lake Forest, known variously as Eastwood Lake, Granny's Lake, or Grandma's Lake, was a natural draw for children. Kids would dare one another to crawl through giant drainpipes, jump from retaining walls into the water, and walk over the dam. Older kids sailed and fished on the lake. One former resident (who prefers to remain anonymous) recalls, "It was a special thrill to sneak over to the lake to swim at night, but I was greatly embarrassed when the police caught a group of us skinny-dipping. The police didn't charge us, just sent us on our way."

The adventures of neighborhood children sometimes took them far from home, occasionally all the way uptown, although Strowd Hill (Franklin Street from Estes Drive to the campus area) made for a daunting uphill climb. A closer and more frequent destination was Eastgate Shopping Center, whose first stores appeared just as the first homes in Coker Hills were being built. All of the land between Eastgate and the Franklin Street bridge over Bolin Creek was undeveloped, so the stores at Eastgate were the closest places to shop. In Eastgate's earliest days, former UNC basketball standout Lennie Rosenbluth operated a bowling alley out of the building that currently houses Trader Joe's, and there was a drive-in movie theater across the street where the Chapel Hill University Inn (formerly the Holiday Inn) now stands.

Several Eastgate stores are vividly remembered by children of that era: Eastgate Hardware, W. T. Grant's Five and Dime,

Wood's, Mann's Drugstore, and, best of all, Billy Arthur's Hobby Shop. The hardware store was owned and operated by Dale and Claudia Evarts' family, so neighborhood children could count on a friendly greeting there. The big draw at Mann's was the counter milkshakes that tasted especially good after a long walk. At Grant's Five and Dime, children could look at the fish and birds sold in the back of the store and browse through bins of candy in the front. Billy Arthur's featured big glass cases with buttons to push to make the shelves revolve, craft supplies of every kind, and a room-sized track where kids paid a quarter to race slot cars. Coker Hills children could walk to Eastgate on a path from Old Oxford Road that came out on Milton Avenue, where they crossed Franklin Street near the site of the original WCHL building. Bikes made for a much faster trip, at least on the way there. Dale Evarts recalls a particularly memorable ride with his sister, Claudia.

"My sister and I were riding our bikes from our house at the north end of Elliott Road to Eastgate, which was downhill the whole way. It was winter and cold, and I hadn't brought gloves or a hat, so I put my head in my jacket and told my sister to yell if a car drove our way. The next thing I knew I was on the hood of a parked car. I yelled at my sister, "Why didn't you tell me that car was there?" When Claudia finally stopped laughing, she replied, "You didn't say anything about parked cars!"

Children roamed the neighborhood at will and thought nothing of cutting through someone's yard, as practically every yard was seen as a highway to somewhere interesting to explore. Construction sites were a favorite for exploration, as kids clambered about half-built homes after crews left for the day. These forays helped Coker Hills kids develop a keen eye as architectural critics, having seen enough houses being built to form strong opinions about what they did and did not like. When they weren't critiquing, they busied themselves seeking the myriad treasures that could be found at these sites, the best of which were empty Coke bottles that could be returned to the A&P for two cents a bottle refund.

All was not fun and games, however; children did have to go to school five days a week. Estes Hills Elementary opened on Estes Drive in 1958 and served the neighborhood children. In the neighborhood's earliest days, older kids attended junior high and high school on West Franklin Street, where University Square once stood. Then, in 1963, Guy B. Phillips Junior High (now Phillips Middle School) opened next door to Estes Hills Elementary School. Chapel Hill High moved to its present location off Homestead Road in 1966, with townspeople complaining mightily because it was so far out in the country.

Children walked or rode their bikes to Estes Hills and Phillips. In the mornings, most kids traveled in groups, picking up friends as they neared the school, so that the journey to and from school was an important social time. No one, except perhaps Boy Scouts on hikes, used backpacks in those days. Kids carried their books and notebooks and complained mightily about how heavy they all were. Bicycles had baskets over the rear wheel, which made a bike ride the easiest way to travel. For walkers, the most direct route was to go straight from the end of North Elliott through the woods to the playground behind Estes Hills Elementary. So many children tromped through there that they quickly wore a path through the underbrush. Eventually, the path was paved and is still used by Coker Hills children today.

In the winter, everyone fervently hoped for a snowstorm that would close school. When one of those few glorious days occurred, the neighborhood kids headed to The Circle or to Curtis Road for memorable sledding runs. Curtis featured a fabulous ride with a long walk back. Curtis was usually plowed before Clayton so the kids had to be quick to sled there. Snow generally remained on Clayton until it melted. Still vivid in the minds of former residents of the neighborhood are the memories of bonfires built on The Circle during these snow days. Children warmed their hands, toasted marshmallows, and talked long past dark. So many bonfires were burned on The Circle, that for many years, pockmarks from those fires could still be seen in the pavement.

What was an idyllic time for children in Coker Hills was also a turbulent time in the world at large. On a sunny November Friday afternoon in 1963, as neighborhood kids were eagerly anticipating the annual Beat Dook parade on Franklin Street, word came that President Kennedy had been assassinated. Susan Prothro remembers riding her bike home from school down North Elliott Road when Ed Hobson burst from his house with his transistor radio in hand, shouting the news. Just two years earlier, most of Coker Hills' kids had seen Kennedy speak at Kenan Stadium on University Day, and it was hard to reconcile the optimism of that day with this national tragedy.

As the civil rights movement took hold, Chapel Hill, like most of the South, struggled with issues of integration. There were a few African-American students at Estes Hills when it opened, but it wasn't until 1966 that the schools became fully integrated. Many neighborhood parents took an active role in the movement, and children remember it as a time of passion and division. Such issues were brought home to Coker Hills in 1968 when the Inter-Church Council (precursor to the Inter-Faith Council) sought to build low-income housing on North Elliott Road. Some neighbors were opposed, while others argued fervently in favor. In the end, the housing was built, and the apartments still stand today behind the Church of Reconciliation.

The earliest residents of Coker Hills embraced the cultural revolution that swept the country in the mid-1960s. Music was an expression of that revolution. Transistor radios accompanied kids on their adventures through the neighborhood, almost always tuned to WKIX in Raleigh. Children made the trip uptown to the Record Bar on Franklin Street to buy the latest record, usually a 45-rpm because an album was too expensive to purchase. When a local Chapel Hill boy was signed by the Beatles' new Apple Records, it was the talk of the neighborhood. That musician, James Taylor, went on to make quite a name for himself.

The turmoil of the times inspired moments of deep conversation during quiet periods of respite. Sarah Geer looks back: "I remember lots of summer evenings lying on our backs and looking at the stars. Since most of the yards were wooded, we couldn't do this in our yards. Instead, we'd lie on the narrow grass verges by the street or at the playground, and watch the bats swoop around the streetlights." Skip Via, too, recalls those contemplative times, summing up nicely the connections that were forged on the streets of Coker Hills and that remain strong in the hearts of its earliest residents. "As the years passed, the games turned more toward very long and thoughtful discussions. We spent a lot of time on our backs, looking at the clouds or the stars, solving all of the world's problems. We were all very good friends, without any sort of cliquishness or overriding social order. Growing up in Coker Hills will remain very special times. Most of us could go lie on our backs in the driveway and continue those conversations now, over fifty years later, and not miss a beat."

**Neighborhood Holiday Caroling
(Left-Right: Michelle Masson, Teresa Gill, Star Gardner and Karen Masson Kendig)**
Photo Courtesy of Michelle Masson

Children at play in Coker Hills
Photo Courtesy of The Masson Family

7//Neighborhood Advocacy

You may never know what results come of your actions, but if you do nothing, there will be no results. — Mahatma Gandhi

Coker Hills has remained a pleasant neighborhood, in part because of neighborhood advocacy efforts. Over the years, neighbors have worked together to preserve and protect the quality of life for the neighborhood. Leading these advocacy efforts has been the Coker Hills Neighborhood Association (CHNA) and Board Members, especially the late Ed Hinsdale, the late Gordon Steele, Barbara Rodbell, and Dan McCauliffe. Absent several successful campaigns and robust leadership from the CHNA Board and members, Coker Hills would be a much different neighborhood. Cars could be racing up and down North Elliott Road even faster than they do today. And rather than being bordered by the Franklin Grove neighborhood with its old oak trees, natural landscaping, stonewalls and brick townhomes, we might have a 24/7 Kroger superstore, generating noise and traffic throughout the neighborhood.

In a past neighborhood meeting about the possible difficulties of a new development, a homeowner expressed concern that protests never did any good. However, actions in Coker Hills show that protest and advocacy can work. Little by little, petition by petition, speech by speech at Town Council meetings, Coker Hills neighbors and the neighborhood association have worked successfully to maintain the quality of life in the neighborhood. Several examples of advocacy follow.

With special appreciation to Patty Krebs, researcher and author of this chapter.

Pritchard Park

Now the site of the Chapel Hill Public Library and Pritchard Park, the Pritchard property comprised about thirty acres of woodlands bordering Coker Hills. In 1983, rumors about a possible development on the land caused concern for the neighborhood. CHNA submitted a petition to the Town Council signed by 158 residents of Coker Hills on November 21 of that year. The purpose of the petition was to support low-density development on the Pritchard property. Patty Krebs, CHNA Vice President, told the Town Council that the Coker Hills petitioners believed a high-density development on this property would have a negative impact on Coker Hills by creating further traffic congestion and impacting the public schools, fire stations and public safety. The CHNA argued that the preservation of an established neighborhood contributed to a sound development plan and to the character of the Town. Why should rezoning to a higher allowable density be permitted if it could put an existing Chapel Hill neighborhood at risk?

A resident of the Estes Hills neighborhood also submitted a petition with over 100 signatures to the Town Council signed by neighbors in support of low-density development. Like the Coker Hills' neighbors, the Estes Hills' petitioners believed high-density development on this property would add to traffic congestion, reduce property values, and destroy the low/high-density ratio recommended for this area by the town's Comprehensive Land Use Plan. Gordon Steele, CHNA Board Member at the time, spoke for the neighborhood in a letter to the Mayor and Town Council dated January 20, 1988: "Not only is this site the geographic center of town but ... with its trees and woods, serves as a much needed passive greenway for this part of town."

With the petitions and other advocacy, interest in developing the land ended and the Pritchard property remained undeveloped for another five years. Then on April 25, 1988, the Town Council announced its intention to purchase the Pritchard property for a sum of $1,050,000 to allow the Town to build a new public library and a community park.

While writing this chapter, the author conducted a telephone interview with William G. Pritchard, Jr., who confirmed that he and the other owners of the Pritchard property would have developed the property had they not sold it. "We didn't want to give it up." he said, "but the city could have exercised eminent domain, and we didn't want to fight them on it. So we worked out a deal. We accepted the town's offer, and our family donated $100,000 to the town for improvements to the proposed park."

On June 27, 1988, the neighboring woodlands were officially named Pritchard Park in memory and in honor of the Pritchard family. The Town Council noted the Pritchard family had owned the land for over fifty years, and the Pritchard name went far back in Chapel Hill history. Pritchard Lane in downtown Chapel Hill is named for the family, and William N. Pritchard was the Mayor of Chapel Hill from 1887 to 1888. CHNA was grateful to the town for negotiating the purchase of the Pritchard land and developing it for a public library and park. Pritchard Park remains today a thirty-acre preserved woodland with beech, poplar, ironwood, and pine trees.

Since the original construction of the public library in 1993, a newer and larger library opened in 2013, on the same site with a slightly larger footprint. The flora, fauna, native species, and wildlife of Pritchard Park remain as a treasure that hopefully the neighborhood and the town will continue to preserve and protect.

Traffic Calming

As growth continued in and around Coker Hills, it became evident to many neighbors that something needed to be done to slow traffic on North Elliott Road. The street had become a favorite short cut to other areas of town, and speeding traffic made it unsafe for pedestrians and for residents backing out of their driveways. In 1986, CHNA asked the town for stop signs on North Elliott Road at Audubon, Michaux, and Velma to help reduce the speed of traffic in the neighborhood.

On March 3, 1986, Town Manager David Taylor denied the CHNA's request for stop signs and shared his rationale for his decision in a memo to the Mayor and Town Council. The Town Manager believed stop signs would result in increased travel time for drivers and would only be effective if placed at close intervals, but the resulting stops and starts would increase congestion and air pollution. Another concern was that the installation of stop signs on North Elliott Road could increase rear-end accidents. The stop signs might also promote increased traffic on adjacent streets, as drivers found routes with fewer stop signs. The Town Manager also cited the Manual of Uniform Traffic Control Devices for Streets and Highways, published by the US Department of Transportation, which discouraged the use of stop signs for speed control.

Given these concerns, the CHNA felt it would have to overcome substantial obstacles to prevail in their campaign for the stop signs. But, prevail they did. CHNA evidenced strong support for their position by submitting a petition signed by over 125 neighborhood residents. The petition read:

Petition to Protect Coker Hills Residential Area from Excessive and Speeding Traffic: We, the undersigned residents of Coker Hills, for reasons of restoring safety and tranquility to our neighborhood by eliminating the use of North Elliott Road as a thoroughfare, petition for stop signs to be installed on North Elliott Road, at Velma, Michaux, and Audubon Road.

A North Elliott Road neighbor, William Murphy, Constitutional Law Professor at the University of North Carolina, School of Law, spoke in favor of the petition. Neighbor and attorney Patty Krebs turned to a US Supreme Court case in arguing the neighborhood's position, Memphis v. Greene, 451 U.S. 100 (1981). This was a case about closing a neighborhood street used by drivers to reduce their commuting time. The neighborhood requested the closing to reduce the flow of traffic using subdivision streets, increase resident safety, and reduce noise and air pollution. In deciding in favor of the neighborhood, the US Supreme Court noted that proper management of vehicular traffic within a city requires accommodating a number of conflicting interests, among them motorists' interests in having unhindered access to their destination, residents' interests in relative quiet, and pedestrians' interest in safety. The Court noted local governments necessarily exercise wide discretion in making policy decisions to accommodate these interests. The Court ruled that the interests of tranquility and safety were unquestionably legitimate and substantial enough to justify an adverse impact on motorists who may be somewhat annoyed by traffic-calming procedures. This was essentially the rationale of CHNA's request to the town, to favor the residents' interests in safety and tranquility despite the minor inconven- ience for some motorists.

After hearing arguments from citizens in the neighborhood, the Town Council rejected the Manager's decision and approved the CHNA stop sign request. After the stop signs were installed, a number of residents observed that traffic speeds had definitely been reduced on North Elliott Road. The neighborhood continues to be concerned with motorists who roll through the stop signs, and CHNA continues to work with the Chapel Hill Police Department on this issue. Recently, several residents took the initiative to place signs reading "Drive like your kids live here" along neighborhood streets.

Kroger

Coker Hill's longest-running advocacy effort was undertaken against the Kroger Company. In 1987, Kroger submitted plans to the town to build a new superstore. Although the company already had a store in Chapel Hill, on the site of what is now Whole Foods, it wished to expand its Chapel Hill presence. These early plans were rejected by the Town, but Kroger re-submitted plans in 1989 (also rejected) and once again in 1995.

In anticipation of eventually getting approval for a new store, Kroger purchased options on acres of land on East Franklin Street, across from what is now Staples. This land was zoned residential and included a windswept meadow under towering old oak trees, where daffodils bloomed in over-grown and long forgotten gardens. Certainly, this land could not remain vacant forever, but the neighborhood never expected a proposal for a commercial development on this site. Kroger proposed a 24/7 "mega" store, nearly double the size of their existing store across Franklin Street. The proposed site would include a 54,762-square-foot building, impermeable surface parking for 290 cars, exterior lights, and potential deliveries during early morning and late night hours.

Not surprisingly, the residents of Coker Hills looked skeptically at the original drawings of the proposed store design, drawings that included a surprising number of mature trees. A member of the Town Council wryly pointed out that some developers included so many trees in their proposal drawings that you could hardly see where the desired buildings might go. This led one wag to ask whether the proposal was for an arboretum. Once again, CHNA board members and neighbors went house-to-house gathering signatures on a petition that read:

"We, the undersigned, residents and voters of Chapel Hill, strongly oppose the Kroger plan to build a new supermarket in the grove of oaks across from Lowe's on East Franklin Street. We urge that their application for a special use permit be denied and the present residential zoning be retained. This move would cause dangerous traffic congestion in the immediate vicinity. It would adversely impact public safety relative to the firehouse, ambulance station, school bus stop, and day care center. It would greatly increase traffic in the neighborhood. Finally, the proposed 24 hour mega supermarket would disrupt the tranquility of the neighboring established residential areas: particularly Elliott Woods, Milton Road, and Coker Hills."

CHNA eventually obtained more than 700 petition signatures and on July 3, 1987, the petition was submitted to the Chapel Hill Town Council. Gordon Steele, a CHNA Board Member, told the Council the proposed superstore would generate impossible traffic along East Franklin and North Elliott Road. Additionally, the driveway for the ambulance and fire station could be blocked, preventing prompt responses to emergencies. The superstore would be only 50 feet from the Elliott Woods Apartments, home to nearly forty families. Steele also noted the exterior lighting for the superstore and the noise from the unloading of trucks had the potential to disturb neighbors at all hours.

Perhaps most telling, Steele asked whether Kroger could claim a neighborhood need for the store. This was required by the Chapel Hill Development Ordinance for the issuance of the special use permit the company was requesting. Steele told the Town there appeared to be no need for another store as proposed by Kroger and quoted from the Town of Chapel Hill Ordinance, Section 8.8.7.1:

"It is the intent of these regulations to provide for development of such commercial centers...to serve areas not already conveniently and adequately provided with commercial and service facilities of the kind proposed."

Steele noted that Chapel Hill already had three supermarkets (Harris Teeter, A&P, and Food Lion) as well as the present Kroger, all within a half-mile radius of the planned superstore. A week later, Steele told the *Chapel Hill News* that he hoped Kroger would realize they had made a stupid decision, and they would decide to back out of their plans.

Indeed, Kroger abandoned this development plan shortly thereafter. However, two years later, in 1989, the company returned with another rezoning request that did not differ substantially from the former request, according to the *Chapel Hill Herald*. In a justification filed with the Planning Board, Kroger argued that the proposed store "should prove to be a captivating addition to East Franklin Street." "This will be a very beautiful project," claimed L. Franklin Childers, real estate manger for Kroger's mid-Atlantic regional office, in an interview with the *News and Observer*. "We're going to maintain a wide buffer along Franklin Street and save the big oak trees. The landscaping will be quite extensive."

In a design drawing, the proposed Kroger building looked like a large warehouse. CHNA President, Barbara Rodbell, commented in a *News and Observer* article that ". . . if there are any people who are for Kroger moving to a new and larger site, I have not met them."

In its application, Kroger also included an analysis of the impact on area traffic compiled by Kimley Horn engineers. Members of the CHNA believed the neighborhood needed their own impact study, but the cost for such a report could be upwards of $1000. Once again, going house-to-house, the CHNA raised funds for a more complete traffic impact evaluation, undertaken by engineer Paul D. Cribbins, P.E. The traffic data from the Kroger report were reviewed. Both reports agreed with the projection of 6,400 daily vehicle trips generated by the proposed development. But Cribbins' further analysis indicated that Kroger's proposed turn lanes and entrances from East Franklin Street and North Elliott Road would be far too short. The Cribbins' report concluded that traffic entering and exiting the proposed site would create serious delays especially during peak traffic periods. Cars wanting to turn left into the Kroger lot and waiting for westbound traffic to pass could block cars waiting to turn left from the intersection. In addition to traffic delays, the proposed road length would not support the predicted additional traffic. Cribbins' study demonstrated that the proposed development would require much longer lanes at the intersection of East Franklin Street and North Elliott Road. The report also concluded that there would likely be more congestion and more accidents than suggested in the Kroger report.

In a letter to the *Chapel Hill News*, CHNA President Barbara Rodbell wrote, "We have many commercial areas in Chapel Hill and not one of them is fully occupied. The proliferation of a commercial enterprise into a residential neighborhood would set a very bad precedent for all of Chapel Hill. This is not just our fight, but it concerns all citizens who value their neighborhoods." On June 6, 1989, the Chapel Hill Project Design Review Board concluded it would not support the Kroger proposal, since it failed to meet standards for approval required by the Town Council. The standards included a requirement that any development maintain or enhance the value of adjacent property and be a public necessity. The staff noted that the Kroger project directly abutted residential property by siting a commercial building too close to residential property lines. The review board criticized the proposal for being insensitive to the surrounding neighborhood. The CHNA argued successfully that this site required, at a minimum, a customized architectural solution, not a generic big-box building design.

Between the project not meeting the town standards and the protests from the neighborhood, Kroger abandoned the proposal. Although Kroger pulled the controversial plans to build a new superstore, the company returned with yet another plan for the same site. This time, however, Kroger purchased adjacent property to allow them to create an intersection with an entrance across from the Eastgate Shopping Center entrance. The new plan also included a nature walk, jogging path with picnic tables, and the store would no longer be opened 24/7.

During a CHNA neighborhood meeting on July 12, 1995, CHNA Board Member Dan McCauliffe formulated a new approach for dealing with what had become an on-going Kroger issue. The CHNA formed the Kroger Property Development Committee. Dan served as the Chair of the committee and other members included Ed LaCombe, Rudy Juliano, Roy Lindahl, Barbara Rodbell, and Patty Krebs. Committee members met frequently with town planning officials and spoke often at meetings with the Town Planning Board and Council. Additionally, the Committee wrote letters to the Planning Board and Council. Committee members worked tirelessly on this effort while simultaneously holding full-time professional positions and managing family lives. This advocacy campaign ran through 1996, when Kroger finally gave up on their development plan for the Franklin Street property. Eventually a residential development, Franklin Grove, was approved for this property. The beautiful old oak trees on the land were protected and preserved, and they continue to enhance the surrounding area.

Neighborhood Conservation District (NCD)

When Dr. Totten asked the Town of Chapel Hill to rezone Coker Hills from agricultural to residential, he requested that the neighborhood have the most restrictive zoning. This request was granted to Coker Hills, but in the mid-1980's, the Town of Chapel Hill rezoned many neighborhoods, including Coker Hills to R-1. However, the town's R-1 zoning requirements were at odds with the neighborhood's restrictive covenant. For example, R-1 allowed for building on .4 acres, a front setback of 28 feet, and 14-foot side setbacks. Not only were the new zoning standards out of compliance with the Coker Hills Restrictive Covenant, but the town could provide a homeowner with a building permit based on the town's zoning requirements. The neighborhood association and/or neighbors then had the responsibility to enforce the more restrictive requirements as stated in the covenant. The CHNA realized that their role as an association should not include being the "covenant police" for the neighborhood. CHNA was not at all pleased to be in the position of having to enforce a legal covenant among neighbors or to incur the possible legal costs and time of doing so.

In 2003, the Town of Chapel Hill passed the Chapel Hill Land Use Management Ordinance (LUMO). For the first time, a town ordinance included the designation of a Neighborhood Conservation District (NCD). The option to apply for an NCD was established, because the town recognized that within Chapel Hill there were residential neighborhoods that contribute significantly to the character and identity of the town and that were worthy of additional preservation and protection. The NCD process was designed to give neighborhoods the opportunity to preserve, protect, and perpetuate the character and identity of their neighborhoods. The topic of the NCD was discussed at a CHNA Board meeting, and the Board made the decision to learn more about this designation and the extent to which it might preserve the character of Coker Hills. The Board formed a committee to study the issue and upon much reflection, the committee recommended that CHNA pursue such a distinction for Coker Hills. In this process, CHNA worked closely with the town planning department. The first requirement directed by the town was to submit a petition reflecting that a majority of neighbors supported the NCD process. During the summer of 2004, a petition was distributed to the neighborhood that stated:

"We, the undersigned owners, petition the Town of Chapel Hill to allow Coker Hills to be designated as a Neighborhood Conservation District and that a neighborhood conservation plan be established through consultation between the Chapel Hill Planning Department and the property owners of Coker Hills."

A majority of Coker Hills' owners signed the petition and the NCD process began. Over the next year, NCD meetings were held by the CHNA and the town to discuss and draft the NCD document. Neighbors were notified of these meetings by the town and by CHNA with mailings and emails. Childcare was provided for some meetings.

The town contracted with Clarion Associates to facilitate the meetings and allowed for neighbors to contact Clarion directly for additional information or for follow-up questions. In February 2006, Clarion Associates presented the Town Planning Board with a Final Recommendation Report for the Coker Hills NCD. By this time, several other Chapel Hill neighborhoods, including Northside and Pine Knolls had already received their NCD approval. Other neighborhoods, like Morgan Creek/Kings Mill and Greenwood started their NCD designation process about this same time. As Greenwood and Morgan Creek moved to receive their NCD approval, Coker Hill's approval was stalled when some neighbors came forward with a petition to delay the Coker Hills NCD due to concerns about some of the NCD conditions.

The town directed CHNA to return to the drawing board and spend time providing additional NCD information to property owners. Further meetings were held to discuss the importance and benefits of the NCD designation. A new neighborhood NCD Committee was established comprising those opposed to and supportive of the NCD. With much additional time and effort an NCD designation for Coker Hills was finally negotiated, agreed upon by all neighborhood parties, and approved by the town. The effective date for the NCD was 2008 and was the sixth approved NCD in Chapel Hill. The Coker Hills NCD (Appendix 2) now serves as a zoning overlay that the town recognizes. The NCD requirements are not identical to those included in the original Restrictive Covenant, but the contents of the NCD are more closely aligned with the original covenant than with the weaker R-1 zoning.

Over the past decades, neighbors have contributed countless volunteer hours in the name of neighborhood advocacy. Board members of the CHNA and neighborhood volunteers have worked together to maintain the character of this neighborhood. Hopefully, as new neighbors move into Coker Hills, they too will devote their time and effort to the continuing protection and improvement of the neighborhood by advocating for Coker Hills. As Richard Moe, President of the National Trust for Historic Preservation once said, "No one says that older neighborhoods should be frozen in time like museum exhibits. The challenge is to manage change so that it does not destroy the distinctive character that makes older neighborhoods so appealing. This means people must take action instead of just sitting back and letting a place we call home be destroyed."[1]

---

[1] *Richard Moe, President's Note, National Trust for Historic Preservation, September/October 2006, page 7.*

Afterword

The environment in which we live deserves our care and attention, and it will take all of us working together to preserve it.
— Tony Wrenn and Elizabeth Mulloy, *America's Forgotten Architecture*

Every neighborhood and house in a neighborhood has a story to tell. This is certainly true of Coker Hills, an historic neighborhood by definition; over fifty years old with many architecturally significant homes. The Coker Hills project began as a modest attempt to learn something about the history of the neighborhood. But like many research and writing projects, it has taken on a life of its own. As more discoveries, stories, and information emerged during the research, it became clear they needed to be included in this book.

Coker Hills, a botanists' neighborhood, is more than just another neighborhood. Coker Hills, with a rich environment and unique history, also has a legacy of neighbors being neighborly. Over the years, neighbors have befriended and cared for one another. Some neighbors have become like extended family and childhood friendships have lasted a lifetime. May this legacy continue.

A neighborhood, sometimes referred to as the "backdrop" of our lives, is an important third "link" in our societal structure; ourselves, family and neighborhood. Drs. Coker and Totten appreciated the importance of this "backdrop." For Dr. Coker, the natural surroundings improved our well-being and lifted our souls. For Dr. Totten, Coker Hills was developed with a sensitivity to preserve as much of the natural beauty as possible. For the reader, I hope there is a new sense of enlightenment and appreciation for the efforts which have made our neighborhood a special place. We do live, however, during a time when older, historic neighborhoods can be forgotten and overlooked by the larger community, where environmental issues are not considered, and the "new" does not fit peacefully with the historic. Owners, future owners, and town leaders will hopefully continue to appreciate historic Coker Hills, a neighborhood which deserves our protection, preservation, care and attention.

Jill Ridky-Blackburn
November 1, 2016

About the Chapel Hill Historical Society

The Chapel Hill Historical Society was founded in 1966 with the mission to research and document local history. The Society provides encouragement and assistance in the study of local history and provides public programs and publications related to the heritage of the area. A volunteer Board of Directors provides oversight of the organization. Volunteers and tax deductible donations are important to the sustainability of the organization. Donations are greatly appreciated.

Chapel Hill Historical Society
PO Box 9032
Chapel Hill, NC 27515-9032

Appendix

Appendix 1

Restrictive Covenant Agreement for Restrictions Applicable to Coker Hills, Chapel Hill, N.C.

Recorded in Plat Book 9, Pages 18 & 19
Orange County Registry

KNOW ALL MEN BY THESE PRESENTS, that The Board of Trustees of Coker College for Women, Founded by J. L. Coker, deceased, do hereby covenant and agree with all persons purchasing properties from it within the area set out below that all lots in the area set out below are subjected to the following covenants and restrictions as to the use thereof, running with said properties by whomsoever owned, and which said restrictions shall be referred to and included by reference in all deeds made and executed by them for properties within said area, to wit:

1. The area to which these restrictions are applicable and binding is as follows: All of the area belonging to the Board of Trustees of Coker College for Women, Founded by J. L. Coker, deceased, lying East of Estes Hills Development, Board of Education of Orange County properties on which is located Estes Hill School and bounded also on the South by said school properties, on the West by property of C.L. Lindsay heirs, on the North by the property of Monroe Partin & Green Johnson heirs, on the North by Lake Forest Estates Development and others, on the East by Vernon L. Crook, the road leading from U.S. Highway 15-501 alternate (Old Chapel Hill to Durham Highway) to the Old Oxford Road, on the South by E.S. Robinson, Old Oxford Road and W. Grady Pritchard et al, known as Coker Hills, Chapel Hill, North Carolina, which is more particularly described by plat recorded in Plat Book 9, at Pages 18 & 19, Orange County Registry.

2. The minimum area of a lot sold for building property shall be six-tenths (0.6) acre. This restriction shall not be interpreted to apply to any area set aside as park.

3. The minimum cost of dwelling structures within this area shall be FIFTEEN THOUSAND ($15,000.00) DOLLARS, exclusive of land cost.

4. Only one dwelling or replacement thereof shall be placed upon each lot. This shall not preclude the sale of tracts by it with the specification as to the number of dwellings that may be placed thereon provided the minimum area as specified in paragraph (2) above is not violated. Nor shall this be interpreted as denying contiguous property owners the right to exchange or sell to each other small strips or areas of their land for the purpose of improving the shape or dimensions of their lots, provided the area restrictions of paragraph (2) above is not violated; and provided further, that any area exchanged shall be added to and become a part of the lot to which it is an addition and subject to the same restrictions as a part of the lot added to and does not increase the number of dwelling lots already provided for said added to lot.

5. No structure shall be erected, altered, placed, or permitted to remain on said property nearer than fifty (50) feet to any of the roads within the area, nor nearer than twenty-five (25) feet to the side or rear lines of the lot.

6. Residential buildings constructed in this area shall be limited to single-family units. This does not preclude nurseries, gardens, schools, fire stations, parks, churches, country clubs, and buildings incidental thereto. No duplex houses, apartments, commercial or industrial buildings shall be constructed within the area. This shall not be interpreted to preclude the provision of servant's quarters or rooms incidental to residence and garage structure, nor does it preclude the inclusion of two or three rooms for rent or one small light housekeeping apartment within the residential structure.

7. No trailer, tent, shack, garage, or other outbuilding erected on a lot shall at any time be used as a residence temporarily or permanently.

8. No cows or hogs may be kept and no barns or hog pens may be constructed on property within the area.

9. No dwelling house, building or other structure shall be erected, placed, or altered on any building lot in this area until the building plans and specifications, and plot plan showing the location of said building, have been approved in writing as to conformity and harmony of exterior design with existing structures in the area, and as to location of the building with respect to topography and the finished ground elevation by a majority of committee composed of Louise V. Coker, H.R. Totten, William Joslin, The Secretary and the Treasurer of Coker College for Women, Founded by J.L. Coker, or by a representative designated by a majority of the members of the said committee. In the case of death, resignation or inability to serve of any member of said committee, the vacancy created shall be filled by appointment by the President of the Board of Trustees of Coker College for Women, Founded by J.L.Coker; and pending such appointment, the surviving member of members or the designated representative or the committee shall have authority to approve or disapprove such design or location. If the aforesaid committee or its authorized representative fails to approve or disapprove a design or location within thirty days after plans have been submitted to it in writing, or in any event, if no suit to enjoin the erection, placement or alternation of such building has been commenced prior to the completion thereof, such approval of said design or location so submitted will not be required. Said committee shall act and serve until the 15th day of September, 1990, at which time the then record owners of a majority of the lots which are subject to the covenants herein set forth may designate in writing duly recorded in the Office of the Register of Deeds of Orange County their authorized representatives who thereafter shall have all the powers subject to the same limitations delegated herein to the aforesaid committee, and for the time limited in said writing. If there is more than one owner of a lot, these owners shall be entitled to only one vote.

10. This agreement shall be made a matter of official record, and its provisions shall be incorporated by reference to the recorded instrument in the deed conveying each parcel of land owned by the Board of Trustees of Coker College for Women, Founded by J.L. Coker, within the area defined herein. These covenants are to run with the land and shall be binding upon all parties and all persons claiming under them until September 15, 1990, after which said covenants shall be automatically extended for successive periods of ten years unless by vote of three-fourths of the then owners of the lots in the area it is agreed

otherwise. These provisions may be amended at any time by the unanimous written agreement of the owners of real estate in this area. All owners of a single lot shall have one (1) vote.

11. Except as specifically limited and permitted above, the zoning ordinances applicable to the most restrictive zone of the Town of Chapel Hill, N.C. now in effect and as hereafter legally enacted and amended shall apply to this area.

12. If the parties hereto, or any of them, or their heirs, successors or assigns, shall violate or attempt to violate any of the covenants herein, it shall be lawful for any of the parties hereto and any of the person or persons owning any real property situated in said development or subdivision to prosecute any proceedings at law or in equity against the person or persons violating or attempting to violate any such covenant to prevent him or them from so doing or to recover damages or other dues for such violation.

13. Invalidation of any one of these covenants by judgment or court order shall in no wise affect any of the other provisions that shall remain in full force and effect.

IN TESTIMONY WHERE OF, the party hereto has caused this restrictive covenant agreement to be sealed within its common seal, signed in it name by its President and attested by its Secretary, the 7th day of September 1960.

THE BOARD OF TRUSTESS OF COKER COLLEGE
FOR WOMEN, FOUNDED BY JAMES L. COKER
BY: Signed by C.W. Coker
President

Appendix 2

COKER HILLS

NEIGHBORHOOD CONSERVATION DISTRICT PLAN

C D - 6

Adopted by the Chapel Hill Town Council October 8, 2007

Effective Date January 1, 2008

SUMMARY

This Coker Hills Neighborhood Conservation District Plan has been prepared and adopted in accordance with Section 3.6.5 in Chapel Hill's Land Use Management Ordinance, and has been incorporated into the Land Use Management Ordinance by reference.

The purpose of a Neighborhood Conservation District is to establish special regulations especially designed for and intended to help preserve the character of a particular, older residential neighborhood. This Plan contains special regulations for the Coker Hills Neighborhood Conservation District (CD-6) as described below.

BOUNDARIES

The boundaries of the Coker Hills Neighborhood Conservation District generally are Clayton Road to the south, Allard Road to the north, Velma Road to the east, and Curtis Road to the west. Please see Attachment 1 for a map of the District boundaries. The boundaries shall be indicated on the official Zoning Atlas which accompanies the Land Use Management Ordinance.

SPECIAL DESIGN STANDARDS TO APPLY TO DEVELOPMENT IN THE COKER HILLS NEIGHBORHOOD CONSERVATION DISTRICT

The following Design Standards shall apply to all development within the Coker Hills Neighborhood Conservation District, and are incorporated into Chapel Hill's Land Use Management Ordinance by reference. No application for development shall be approved that does not comply with these standards. For the Coker Hills Neighborhood Conservation District, these standards replace/supersede general provisions in the Land Use Management Ordinance where such standards differ. For standards that are not specifically identified in this Plan, provisions of the underlying zoning district for a particular parcel shall apply.

The standards for the Coker Hills Neighborhood Conservation District are as follows:

Regulation	Standard for Coker Hills*
Minimum Lot Size	.6 Acre
Maximum Floor Area Ratio for Single- Family Dwelling (or Single-Family Dwelling with Accessory Apartment)	.2
Maximum Size for Single-Family Dwelling (or Single-Family Dwelling with Accessory Apartment)	7,500 square feet
Minimum Street Setback	40 feet
Minimum Interior and Solar Setbacks for Single-Family Dwelling (or Single-Family dwelling with Accessory Apartment)	20 feet for interior and solar setback
Accessory Apartments	Permitted – No additional minimum lot size requirement
Effective Date	January 1, 2008

*For the Coker Hills Neighborhood Conservation District, these standards replace/supersede general, otherwise applicable provisions in the Land Use Management Ordinance where such standards applicable to the property differ. For standards that are not specifically identified in this Plan, provisions of the underlying zoning district for a particular parcel shall apply.

Appendix 3

Coker Hills Original Owners

Lot #	Address	House Name*	Original Homeowner	Land Purchased	Built
1	417 Clayton	Stuart	George E. and Gene Stuart	5/20/69	1971
2	415 Clayton	Rashkis	Melvin F and Zora Rashkis	3/22/63	1967
3	413 Clayton	Lahey	Chris and Christina Lahey	5/20/64	2015
4	411 Clayton	Townend	Marion Townend	2/15/61	1966
4A	N.Elliott/Franklin	CH Fire Station III	Robert and Catherine Cox-prop.owner	5/17/65	1971
5	409 Clayton	Stehman-White Oak	Carlyle John and Ursula Barbara Stehman	6/28/65	1981
6	407 Clayton	Stehman-Trillium	Carlyle John and Ursula Barbara Stehman	4/19/62	1962
7	405 Clayton	Umphlett	Clyde J and Margaret M. Umphlett	12/1/64	1965
8	403 Clayton	Winslow	Rex and Lucille Winslow	1/5/61	1964
9	401 Clayton	Koch	William J. and Dorothy Koch	11/1/63	1964
10	311 Clayton	Rice	Oscar Knefker and Hope Sherfy Rice	7/24/62	1962
11	309 Clayton	Johnston	Charles L.and Majories Johnston,Jr.	11/23/60	1962
12	307 Clayton	Via	Warren W.and Alberta T. Via	4/6/61	1961
13	305 Clayton	Lindahl	Roy and Gwen Lindahl	1/23/61	1965
14-15	1405 Michaux	Hinsdale	Charles E. and Ann Lee Hinsdale	4/26/62	1962
16	1503 Michaux	Wettach	John T. and Josephine Wettach	11/22/60	1963
17	1601 Curtis	Allen	William L. and Frances Allen,Jr	6/11/63	1963
18	1600 Curtis	Neal	Robert S. Neal, Jr.	6/20/63	1965
19	412 Clayton	McGuire	Howell N.and Josephine McGuire	7/18/63	1964
20	410 Clayton	Sluder	Troy Bunyon and Ruth H. Sluder,Jr.	8/3/62	1969
21	408 Clayton	Johnston	Peter R. and Helen Clark Johnston	1/14/64	1964
22	406 Clayton	Bost	W. Thomas and Evelyn B. Bost, Jr.	8/14/61	1962
23	404 Clayton	Pickett	Oscar A.and Fay E. Pickett, Jr.	11/28/60	1963
24	402 Clayton	Davis	Samuel J. and Elizabeth Davis	6/5/63	1963
25	400 Clayton	Fountain	Ben F.and Norma Fountain, Jr	4/6/61	1961
26	na	E.C. Leonard Playground	Coker Hills Playground	6/17/63	na
27	308 Clayton	Dyer	James C. Dyer	2/20/63	1964
28	306 Clayton	Gill	Edward J. and Doris R.Gill	7/11/61	1962
29	304 Clayton	Jennings	Sion D.and Margaret Bowman Jennings	10/25/60	1961
30	1505 Michaux	Anstett	Ethel M. Anstett	10/20/61	1962
31	1603 Curtis	Clements	John B and Sylvia T. Clements	3/25/61	1962
32	415 N. Elliott	Donnan	Pearl and William Donnan	9/6/61	1964
33	413 N. Elliott	Yohe	William O. and Pearl P. Yohe	8/9/61	1962
34	411N. Elliott	Davis	Joseph and Margaret Davis	1/9/61	2004
35	409 N. Elliott	Hobson	Patrick H.and Lydia "Pete" Hobson	11/21/60	1962
36	407 N. Elliott	Clark	Dr. Howard G. and Julia Clark,III	2/18/61	1962
37	405 N. Elliott	McDonald	Sharyn Lynn McDonald	11/2/63	1966
38	403 N.Elliott	Seibel	Paul and Mary J. Seibel	7/27/65	1965
39	401 N. Elliott	Kessing	Jonas W. and Alice H. Kessing	4/19/62	1962
40	311 N. Elliott	Perry	Martha and Frank Perry	4/30/63	1963
41	309 N. Elliott	Masson	James C. and Barbara S.Masson	11/17/60	1961
42	307 N. Elliott	Weaver	Ben F. and Cynthia C. Weaver	4/21/61	1962
43	305 N. Elliott	Tenney	Edwin W. and Anita L. Tenney, Jr.	8/8/61	1962
44	303 N. Elliott	Klinker	William H. and Lois Diane Klinker, Jr.	7/26/62	1962
45	1507 Michaux	Johnson	James E. and Vivian S.Johnson	12/21/60	1962
46	1506 Michaux	Ligon	Ruddy M.and Anne K. Ligon,Jr.	1/17/62	1962
47	211 N. Elliott	Muth	Riman E. and Frances Muth	11/21/64	1967
48	203 Woods Circle	Abbott	R.Max and Mary H. Abbott	4/2/63	1964
49	na	Hill	David W. and Ruth Hill	11/14/62	
50	205 Woods Circle	Hill	David W. and Ruth Hill	11/14/62	1963
51	204 Velma	Sanderford	James L and Mary Sanderford	12/1/66	1966
52-53	1506 Velma	Vickery	Dr. Walter N. and Anne Vickery	4/1/69	1972
54	1502 Velma	Rugen	Carol and David Rugen	9/9/61	1987
55	1500 Michaux	Barton	Roger E. and Dorothy J. Barton	11/28/60	1961
56	1502 Michaux	Bunn	James A. and Dorothy Bunn	5/18/62	1967
57	1504 Michaux	Ward	Ira A.and Caroline B.Ward	12/18/61	1962
58	209 Woods Circle	Tillman	Rollie P. and Mary Windley Tillman	9/25/61	1962
59	207 Woods Circle	Thrasher	Thomas R. and Anna P. Thrasher	4/28/61	1963
60	1701 Curtis	Donnan	Robert and Nancy Donnan	2/22/65	1966
60A	na	Walkway	Walkway to Estes Elementary	8/27/64	na
61	412 N. Elliott	Udry	J. Richard and Janice Udry	5/9/66	1966
62	410 N. Elliott	Carter	Walter C. and Elizabeth B. Carter	11/28/60	1962
63	408 N. Elliott	Waddell	William J.and Audry Chris Waddell	11/28/60	1962
64	406 N. Elliott	Hutchison	Richard R. and Anne Hutchison	3/30/66	1966
65	404 N. Elliott	Byrd	Robert and Patricia Byrd	1/27/66	1968

#	Address	Surname	Owners	Date	Year
66	402 N. Elliott	George	Claude S. and Eleanor George, Jr.	1/27/60	1968
67	400 N. Elliott	Curtis	Thomas E. and Marilou Curtis	4/13/62	1963
68	308 N. Elliott	Cogswell	Arthur and Betty Cogswell	3/22/65	1970
69	306 N. Elliott	Prothro	James W. and Mary Frances Prothro	5/11/61	1962
70	304 N. Elliott	Wysor	Ida Lauch and William G. "Bud" Wysor	8/21/63	1963
71	302 N. Elliott	Floyd	Joe and Josephine Bone Floyd	10/9/63	1965
72	300 N. Elliott	Summer	George K. and Betsy Summer	10/29/63	1966
73	206 N. Elliott	Holmes	Carl B. and Martha Holmes	4/21/64	1964
74	204 N. Elliott	Dearborn	Dewitt Clinton and Hope Dearborn	5/15/64	1965
75	202 N. Elliott	Bouldin	Thomas and Betty Bouldin	12/6/63	1978
76	101 A&B Eastwood Lake	Levin	Charlotte M. and Richard I. Levin	11/2/66	1972
77	1703 Curtis	Leonard	E.C. and Murlie Hinds Leonard	1/6/62	1962
78	1704 Curtis	Philas	Peter G. and Ida L. Philas	7/9/68	1968
79	1704 Curtis	Philas	Peter G. and Ida L. Philas	4/10/65	1968
80	402 Lyons	Whittier	Mary Whittier	6/9/69	1969
81	404 Lyons	Monroe	John T. and Jane K. Monroe	12/19/69	1970
82	406 Lyons	Goodwin	Francis B. Goodwin	5/1/68	1968
83	408 Lyons	Warren	David and Marsha Warren	11/2/66	1973
84	1703 Audubon	Upham	James B. and Majory Upham	10/3/67	1970
85	1702 Audubon	Behrman	Jack Newton and Louise Behrman	3/22/65	1965
86	1703 Allard	Royal	Billy W. and Lil Royal	1/7/64	1967
87	1702 Allard	Taylor	Duane F. and Patricia M. Taylor	3/5/64	1965
88	1703 Michaux	Turner	John Brister and Marian Turner	3/18/64	1971
89	1810 S. Lakeshore	Harper	Charles L. and Katherine H. Harper	3/30/66	1966
90	1808 S. Lakeshore	Pearce	Herbert and Agnes Pearce	7/31/69	1969
91	1806 S. Lakeshore	McLeran	James H. and Virginia A. McLeran	3/12/69	1969
92	1804 S. Lakeshore	Thomas	Dr. Grady and Joy Thomas	8/15/68	1968
93	1802 S. Lakeshore	Bullock	Leonard S. and Jane Bullock	10/13/65	1968
94	1713 Michaux	McLeese	Hugh D. and Evelyn McLeese	8/2/67	1969
95	1703 Allard	Dietz	Alice Dietz	1/6/64	1974
96	1711 Michaux	Stocking	E. Barbara Stocking	7/26/67	1969
97	1709 Michaux	Nelson	James C. Nelson	10/24/67	1968
98	1707 Michaux	Bell	Gerald D. and Christina Bell	7/6/67	1969
99	1705 Michaux	Glenn	Willie L. and Nancy Glenn	8/10/66	1968
100	1702 Michaux	Colwell	Robert E. and Louise Colwell	3/5/64	1964
101	1704 Michaux	Breslin	Marianne S. Breslin- Gaither	4/23/64	1965
102	1706 Michaux	Mauldin	James R. and Genevieve Mauldin	4/16/69	1969
103	1708 Michaux	Hopper	Jerry R. and Kaye Hopper	5/16/68	1968
104	1710 Allard	Hakan	M. Joseph and Joy G. Hakan	10/12/68	1981
105	1710 Michaux	Eastman	Sidney Lewis and Jane Eastman	3/20/68	1968
106	1712 Michaux	Bowles	Victor P. and Doris Bowles	7/24/67	1968
107	1714 Michaux	Choi	Sang-Il and Etsuyo Choi	7/1/67	1972
108	1708 Audubon	Gregg	John H. and Gail D. Gregg	5/7/67	1972
109	1711 Allard	Falk	Jeanette and David Falk	10/1/66	1972
110	1710 Audubon	Hubbard	Paul S. and Sylvia Hubbard	7/13/67	1969
111	1713 Audubon	Locher	Walter E. and Gretchen Locher	5/31/68	1969
112	1711 Audubon	Scott	Tom K. and Harriet (Hattie) Scott	4/25/69	1970
113	1709 Audubon	Autry	George and Bess Autry	9/1/68	1969
114	1707 Audubon	Ball	Dr. Lester and Betty Ball	12/5/67	1970
115	1705 Audubon	Obrist	Paul A. and Ellie Obrist	7/13/67	1968
116	407 Lyons	Etherridge	James E. and Jacqueline Etherridge	1/14/66	1966
117	405 Lyons	Hagadorn	Irvine R. and Martha Hagadorn	12/18/65	1971
118	417 Lyons	Maher	Phillip and Ruth Maher	3/1/67	1969
119	1721 Allard	White	James Rushton and Helen White	12/1/65	1966
120	411 Lyons	Allen	Don Lee and Martha Allen	10/6/63	1964
121	409 Lyons	Gastineau	John Willian and Nova Jeanne Gastineau	3/14/67	1967
122	410 Lyons	Nelson	William and Susan Nelson	1/31/68	1972
123	412 Lyons	Edmands	Elizabeth Merrill Edmands	3/1/67	1968
124	414 Lyons	Akin	Ethel Redney Akin	4/21/66	1967
125	1706 Curtis	Wilkins	John K. and Johnsie Wilkins	10/26/67	1968
126	1708 Curtis	Watkins	Julia Day Watkins	2/10/66	1966
127	1727 Allard	Stowe	Howard D. and Barbara Stowe	5/7/68	1969
128	1732 Allard	Hanst	Phillip and Constance Hanst	10/28/69	1970
129	1730 Allard	Crounse	Marian and Robert Crounse	11/6/65	1972
130	1728 Allard	Sears	Bion and Mary Sears	10/2/68	1973
131	1726 Allard	Stephenson	Robert M. Stephenson, Jr.	12/15/67	1968
132	1724 Allard	Bartlett	Robert B. and Eveleyn M. Bartlett	11/8/67	1971
133	1722 Allard	Cornwell	Robert R. and Joy Cornwell	10/14/67	1972
134A	1720 Allard	Conway	Charles W. Thompson and Eugenia C. Conway	2/29/72	1973

*The information above represents the author's best attempt to be as accurate as possible.

Appendix 4

Coker Hills Lot Map

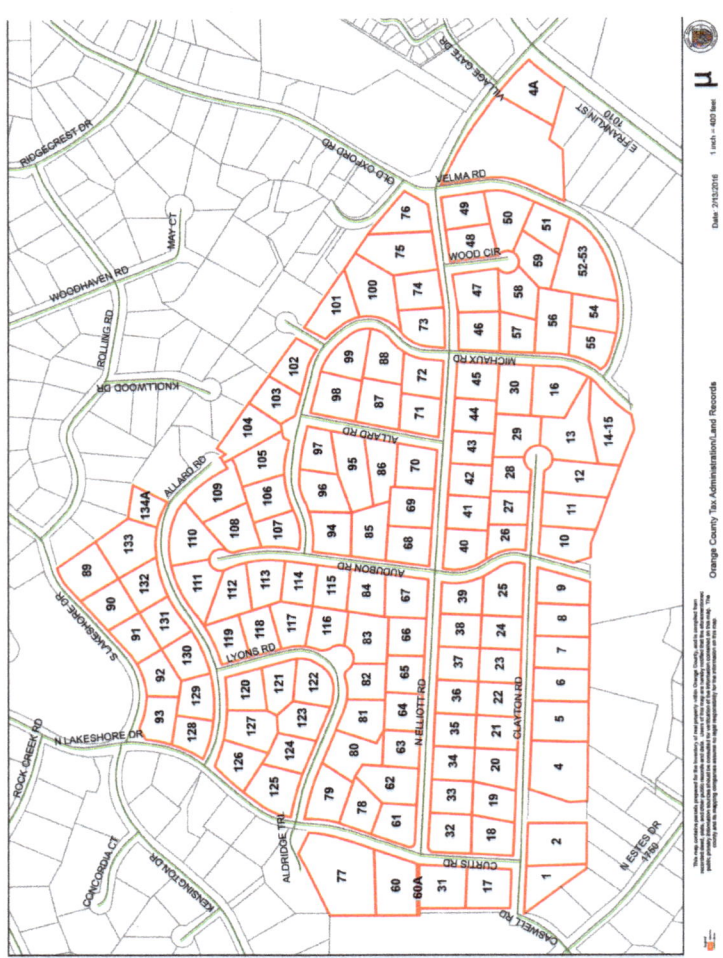

www.ingramcontent.com/pod-product-compliance
Lightning Source LLC
Chambersburg PA
CBHW061216070526
44584CB00029B/3856